AF522236

Human Rights And Peace

By

Dr. M. Lakshmi Narasaiah

M.A., Ph.D.,
Professor and Head
Department of Economics
Sri Krishnadevaraya University
Post-graduate Centre,
Kurnool—518 002
Andhra Pradesh

DISCOVERY PUBLISHING HOUSE
NEW DELHI-110002

First Published-2003

Reprinted-2011

ISBN 81-7141-676-4

Published by

DISCOVERY PUBLISHING HOUSE
4831/24, Ansari Road, Prahlad Street,
Darya Ganj, New Delhi-110002 (India)
Phone: 3279245 • Fax: 91-11-3253475
E-mail:dphtemp@indiatimes.com

Printed at: **Mehra Offset Press, Delhi**

PREFACE

The end of the millennium has seen some remarkable advances in political democracy. Oppressed peoples everywhere are at last, or once again, tasting freedom. They owe these victories largely to themselves, to the intelligence, determination, and even the genius of their citizens.

But this freedom will be fragile as long as it is cast in a single mould, the vehicle of a uniform globalization which speaks with a single voice, primarily that of commerce. Principles may be universal; the mechanisms that infuse life into them are shaped by a host of features that are specific to each society.

No vision of democracy—which transcends politics and includes economic, social and cultural life can—really take root if it is a sterile copy that fails to take account of the history and myths, the values and traditions of each people. While these roots are necessary, however, they provide no justification for citing 'cultural relativism' as an excuse for violating the basic principles on which the rights of human beings are founded. Respect for 'cultural identity' cannot legitimize anti-democratic practices.

A second danger arises from the fact that the field in which these rights are elaborated and exercised is all too often limited. The recent commemoration of the Universal Declaration of Human Rights was a reminder that human rights comprise not only political and civil rights but also, on exactly the same basis, economic and social rights, such as the right to a job, housing, health and education.

One and a half billion people live in a dire poverty. Their most fundamental right, the right to life, the bedrock of all other rights, is constantly threatened. So that still unfinished struggle to extend and strengthen human rights includes the duty to promote development.

This duty is not only a matter of legal formalism or an ethical imperative. Fundamental freedoms will remain very fragile as long as poverty, exclusion and inequalities persist. The forces of globalization encourage the establishment of the rule of law, but a version of law biased in favour of rules needed for successful business activity. They also do more to sharpen economic and social tensions rather than to reduce them.

The momentum created by efforts to establish the rule of law in a growing number of countries is coming up against a major obstacle. The principles and rules that govern international relations are increasing their influence on the lives of nations, but they are very far indeed from being democratic. The strongest still hold sway.

This is true where individual states are concerned. They feel their wings have been clipped, and see their legitimate prerogatives being eroded by the rise of a kind of private-sector absolutism, which tends to limit the functions of government to security and mediation, paralyzing its role as the guarantor of the general interest and depriving it of the necessary means to apply the rule of law.

It is also true of the community of states because there is still no world structure which is accepted as the embodiment of the force of law. The United Nations is a unique international democratic forum, but its authority has been weakened first by nearly half a century of the Cold War and then by unilateral actions taken by the major powers, in defiance of the very principles they profess to defend. The rule of law is indivisible; it must encompass freedom and welfare, individual countries and the world at large.

Dr. M. Lakshmi Narasaiah

CONTENTS

1

All Human Rights for All

The end of the millennium has seen some remarkable advances in political democracy. Oppressed peoples everywhere are at last, or once again, tasting freedom. They owe these victories largely to themselves, to the intelligence, determination, and even the genius of their citizens.

But this freedom will be fragile as long as it is cast in a single mould, the vehicle of a uniform globalization which speaks with a single voice, primarily that of commerce. Principles may be universal; the mechanisms that infuse life into them are shaped by a host of features that are specific to each society.

No vision of democracy—which transcends politics and includes economic, social and cultural life can—really take root if it is a sterile copy that fails to take account of the history and myths, the values and traditions of each people. While these roots are necessary, however, they provide no justification for citing 'cultural relativism' as an excuse for violating the basic principles on which the rights of human beings are founded. Respect for 'cultural identity' cannot legitimize anti-democratic practices.

A second danger arises from the fact that the field in which these rights are elaborated and exercised is all too often limited. The recent commemoration of the Universal Declaration of Human Rights was a reminder that human rights comprise not only political and civil rights but also, on exactly the same basis, economic and social rights, such as the rights to a job, housing, health and education.

One and a half billion people live in dire poverty. Their most fundamental right, the right to life, the bedrock of all other rights, is constantly threatened. So the still unfinished struggle to extend and strengthen human rights includes the duty to promote development.

This duty is not only a matter of legal formalism or an ethical imperative. Fundamental freedoms will remain very fragile as long as poverty, exclusion and inequalities persist. The forces of globalization encourage the establishment of the rule of law, but a version of law biased in favour of rules needed for successful business activity. They also do more to sharpen economic and social tensions rather than to reduce them.

The momentum created by efforts to establish the rule of law in a growing number of countries is coming up against a major obstacle. The principles and rules that govern international relations are increasing their influence on the lives of nations, but they are very far indeed from being democratic. The strongest still hold sway.

This is true where individual states are concerned. They feel their wings have been clipped, and see their legitimate prerogatives being eroded by the rise of a kind of private-sector absolutism, which tends to limit the functions of government to security and mediation, paralyzing its role as the guarantor of the general interest and depriving it of the necessary means to apply the rule of law.

It is also true of the community of states because there is still no world structure which is accepted as the embodiment of the force of law. The United Nations is a unique international democratic forum, but its authority has been weakened first by nearly half a century of the Cold War and then by unilateral actions taken by the major powers, in defiance of the very principles they profess to defend. The rule of law is indivisible; it must encompass freedom and welfare, individual countries and the world at large.

2

Human Rights—The Road to Progress and Peace

The UN Declaration on Human Rights has been fifty years old. A moment is needed to take stock and to look at the deficits which still exist in terms of human rights half a century later. The declaration of 1948 contains a comprehensive list of political, economic, social and cultural rights and aims at the protection of the freedom, equality, and human dignity of all human beings, irrespective of their race, gender, language or religion. Never before in history had there been such a far-reaching and solemn undertaking to protect each and every individual from all forms of oppression and deprivation. Two treaties adopted by the UN General Assembly in 1966 translate the ideas of the Human Rights Declaration into binding international law, and a High Commissioner for Human Rights, an office created as a result of the UN Human Rights Conference in Vienna in 1993, has been put in charge of monitoring the human rights situation and coordinate UN action on it. Numerous human rights NGOs all over the world, most important among them Amnesty International, have established themselves as additional watchdogs to guard against human rights violations.

But inspite of all the attention human rights issues are receiving, especially in the Western democracies, the progress achieved in guaranteeing fundamental human rights to every individual is anything but satisfactory. It is true: with the collapse of fascism and communism, and the disappearance of many of the military regimes in Latin America, Asia and Africa, some of the ugliest tyrants who trampled human rights under their feet have gone. Democratic structures are on the advance, and with them a certain measure of rule of law. In more and more countries, governments are elected by the people which means that they are to some extent accountable to their voters and cannot violate human rights with impunity. However, even where there is formal democracy and elections are periodically being held, social, economic or cultural rights are persistently denied to large groups of people.

In Africa millions of girls are circumcised (female genital mutilation) with grave consequences for their Physical and psychological well being—a serious violation of their human rights although defended by African males as cultural practice. In India, "the world's largest democracy", millions of dalits suffer from discrimination and exclusion because they do not belong to the caste system; tens of millions of children are forced to work under harsh conditions, ruining their health and missing opportunities for education; bonded labours are toiling for rich landowners in rural areas; and girls and women are suppressed by customs which still grant all the economic power to men. There are good laws in India which forbid all these practices; but the laws are not enforced in the absence of strong institutions which reach down to the village level.

This is the situation in many countries: the existing legal framework guarantees the protection of human rights as enshrined in the UN Declaration. But the reality is quite different.

All these are accounts of the daily violations of human rights which are going on in many countries and which throw a long and dark shadow over the human rights. Most of those oppressed and stripped of their rights are poor people, those on the lowest range of the scale. Because they are poor, they find it almost impossible to assert their rights which they may hold under the constitution and the laws of the country in which they live. They are often illiterate and do not even know their rights, and when they do, they have no money to pay a lawyer and to go to court. For many of the more than 1 billion people living in abject poverty, human rights therefore do not exist in reality. They are far from being able to live a life in dignity as demanded by the UN Declaration.

Human Rights, therefore, cannot be protected in isolation from economic and social factors. If we manage to reduce poverty, we will also help to improve the human rights situation. Development policy thus becomes a key to the problem without the enforcement of political human rights, social human rights cannot permanently be secured. On the other hand, the realisation of political human rights depends to a large extent on favourable economic, social and cultural conditions.

Human rights, when denied to people, can be a source of internal or internal conflict—just think of the millions of refugees who had to leave their homes due to ethnic and religious strife. The world would therefore be a safer place if full human rights were granted to all individuals in the world as proclaimed in the UN Declaration fifty years ago. Peace and progress would be the reward if we achieve this noble goal.

3

Speaking from A Position of Economic Strength—The Human Rights Debate and Asia

The recent debate on 'Asian Values' and human rights has developed into a cottage industry. At every turn politicians, academics, and opportunists of all ilks are jumping on the bandwagon giving their version of what human rights are all about and whether Asia should be unique in its approach to human rights issues and its quest for democracy and modernity. Unfortunately, in issues of this kind, the debate attracts all sorts of people, each with their own specific agendas, and neither 'Asian values' proponents nor opponents speak with one voice.

What is perhaps most surprising is how quickly the debate has polarized the camps, reviving the age-old divide between East and West. Taking a step back, however, is it really just cultural differences that separate the two camps I think the real interests underpinning the debate have nothing at all to do with questions of culture, or indeed, even human rights. Rather, they are related to Asian economic success and confidence and Asia's continuing reaction to colonialism.

I doubt very much if this debate would have even started were late twentieth-century Asia nothing but a sea of poverty, degradation and squalor. But it is not. Asia is booming, and economists and analysts alike are calling the next century the

'Pacific Century,' an obvious reference to the tremendous growth in the Asia-pacific region. The Asian 'economic miracle' has been linked to so-called Confucian and Asian values by no less venerable an institution than the World Bank. The linkage between economic growth and cultural values has given Asian leaders and intellectuals a new-found confidence in two ways. First, Asian voices, particularly those emanating from countries, like Singapore, Malaysia, South Korea, Taiwan, and Thailand, are standing up to their detractors with a confidence buoyed by their countries' double-digit growth. Second, economic success cloaks many of these Asian governments in what is called as 'performance legitimacy'. Countries in Asia are modernizing and growing at an unprecedented pace, and Asian leaders and their people are justifiably proud of their achievements. The present Asian Financial crises is temporary.

In the face of such overwhelming success, new-found national pride pits Asian countries against the 'decadent West', which constantly preaches to Asian nations to conform to what it believes to be universally established standards of human rights practice. Constant pressure to observe human rights obligations, often applied with threats of economic sanctions, is regarded by many as a slap in the Asian face and, more importantly, an attempt by the West to hold the East to ransom. Beyond a cursory flat denial of human rights violations, Asians must justify their actions, and one powerful way to do this is by claiming historical, cultural, and religious exception. At the same time some Asian states push the cultural line to support their soft authoritarian form of governments, which have, to gather with their social and economic agendas, also come under attack from western leaders and intellectuals. In this sense, Asian states are really fighting for the right to be modern, not to forge their own version of human rights.

Most Asian scholars very keen on the 'Asian values' debate because it is an opportunity to take on the West in an intellectual exchange where the West does not have a clear and distinct advantage.

The positions the West is taking in the debate are no different from those the West has always stood by. Media coverage in recent years, however, has impassioned the debate and has thus highlighted and, in some respects, shaped the divergence of interests between East and West. The stakes in the debate have come to be planted along civilizational lines that cut deep into the national and hemispheric pride of both parties. When the debate is couched in these terms, then all the other baggage is imported along with it. So I don't believe the West is overreacting in its response to the debate. I do, however, detect a sense of panic among many Western scholars and politicians—result of the fact that many Asians appear to be speaking from a position of strength; strength drawn not from the merits of intellectual arguments but from economic success.

Can the Western response be improved? It's difficult to say. The West is primarily concerned with the merits of the conceptual arguments. While the West is concerned with whether it is at all possible to take a relativist approach to human rights issues, Asia is more concerned with power politics. The East's reaction to this must, I think, be viewed in its proper context. The problem as Asians see it is this: How can the West—especially America—preach democracy and human rights as fundamental values when the West can't even get its own house in order? Asia, on the other hand, is less the hypocrite because it takes a culturally relativist approach to the situation and does not pretend to be the champion of human rights. Such is the view of many in Asia.

It is interesting to note that the human rights debate has without a doubt attracted more scholars, intellectuals, and politicians in the West than in Asia. There are two possible reasons for this. Western liberalism and its ideals are under threat, and this siege on the Western citadel has drawn more and more Western leaders and intellectuals into the fray, compelled to stage a spirited defence against Asia's confident and well-considered alternative world view. But, it could also be true that Asian intellectuals are just having too good a time enjoying their newly acquired wealth to worry so much about such conceptual debates.

4

Safe Motherhood is a Human Rights Issue

The death of a women during pregnancy or childbirth is not only a health issue but also a matter of social injustice. Of the human rights currently acknowledged in national constitutions and in regional and international human rights treaties, many can be applied to safe motherhood. Many such treaties and conventions are based on the 1948 Declaration of Human Rights *(i)* they include the Convention on the Elimination of All Forms of Discrimination against Women; *(ii)* the Convention on the Rights of the Child, *(iii)* the European Convention for the Protection of Human Rights and Fundamental Freedoms; *(iv)* the American Convention on Human Rights *(v)* and the African Charter on Human and Peoples' Right.

Human rights of relevance to safe motherhood can be grouped into the following four principal categories:

- *Rights relating to life, liberty and security of the person,* which require governments to ensure both access to appropriate health care during pregnancy and childbirth, and women's rights to decide whether, when, and how often to bear children. Governments must therefore address factors within the economic, legal, social and health systems that deny women these fundamental rights.

- *Rights relating to the foundation of families and of family life*, which require governments to provide access to health services and other facilities that women need to establish families and to enjoy life within a family.

- *Rights Relating to health care and the benefits of scientific progress, including health information and education*, which require governments to provide access to good sexual and reproductive health care with appropriate referral systems. The measures needed to ensure safe motherhood can be provided through primary health care and irrespective of a country's level of economic development. Central to these rights is information on a range of reproductive health issues, including family planning, abortion, and sex education.

- *Rights relating to equality and nondiscrimination*, which require governments to provide access to services such as education and health care without discriminatory grounds such as sex, martial status, age, and socio-economic class. Discriminatory policies include requirements for a woman to obtain the consent of her husband for particular health care interventions, requirements for parental authorization which have a differential impact on girls, and laws that criminalize medical procedures that only women need. Governments are in violation of their obligations when they fail to implement laws that effectively protect women's interests or to allocate health resources to meet women's particular need for safe pregnancy and childbirth.

The actions that governments need to take to promote safe motherhood as a human right fall into three groups:

- *Reform of laws* that prevent women from attaining the highest possible levels of health and nutrition needed for safe pregnancy and childbirth and that inhibit access to reproductive health information and services such as laws requiring women in need of health care to seek the authorization of husbands or other family members first.

- *Implementation of laws* that foster women's rights to good health and nutrition and that protect women's health interests such as laws that prohibit child marriage, female genital mutilation, rape and sexual abuse. Every effort should be made to implement laws that encourage the healthy timing of birth, such as those that support the education of girls, set a minimum age for marriage, and ensure women's access to essential health care.

- *Application of human rights* in national legislation and policy to advance safe motherhood.

5

A Nuclear Weapon Free World

That Dream Must Become Reality

Until recently the likelihood of achieving a world without nuclear weapons was very, very small. But we are now living in a different world, and in this new configuration, what was a utopian dream yesterday can be the subject of serious discussions today, and put into practice tomorrow.

It was by a quirk of history that the conception of the atom bomb coincided with the start of the Second World War. The main motivation for the scientists who initiated the work on the atom bomb was that the bomb should not be used. Our argument was that we needed the bomb in order to deter Hitler from using his bomb against us. But as it happened our bombs were used, they were used as soon as they were made, and they were used against civilian populations. The bombs on Hiroshima and Nagasaki have brought the Second World War to a rapid end. But they also had another effect, namely they demonstrated to the Soviet Union the newly-acquired, over whelming power of the United States. From the very beginning nuclear weapons were seen as a major tool in the ideological struggle between the United States and the Soviet Union.

With the end of the Cold War, and the collapse of one of the combatants in the world power struggle, a unique opportunity was created for a radical solution to the nuclear-weapon issue. But instead, the nuclear arsenals are being maintained, albeit at reduced levels. The main reason given for this is that nuclear weapons are needed as a safeguard against the potential threat from new nations acquiring these weapons.

Horizontal proliferation is a real danger, but the retention of nuclear weapons as a means of dealing with it is about the worst possible answer. At the heart of horizontal proliferation is the perception that nuclear weapons confer power, prestige and protection. This motivated the earliest proliferators, France and Britain, and is sustained by the fact that the only five permanent members of the Security Council, with right of veto, are the five nuclear weapon states. As long as this nuclear cult exists, as long as the belief is sustained that nuclear weapons bestow status, strength and security, the pressure to join the club will be irresistible.

The main instrument to prevent nuclear proliferation is the Non-Proliferation Treaty. By now 162 states have signed the Treaty, including all five nuclear weapon states. But the NPT is an interim arrangement, step towards nuclear disarmament, as clearly stated in its Preamble. A stable world order must be based on the rule of law, and one cannot imagine an international law that permanently discriminates between nations. If some states are allowed to keep nuclear weapons, because—they claim—they are needed for their security, one cannot deny the acquisition of these weapons to other states.

In the long term, there are only two alternatives: allow the possession of nuclear weapons to all states by eliminating these weapons. There can be no doubt that the former would lead to a highly dangerous, unstable world. The creation of a nuclear-weapon-free world is therefore essential for peace and stability.

A nuclear-weapon-free world is also called for on moral grounds. The whole fabric of civilized society is based on moral values, and if these are violated in one important area, how can they be defended in others? Security achieved by the threat of wholesale destruction, possibly genocide, is bound in the long term to erode the ethical basis of civilization.

Several arguments have been advanced against the idea of a world without nuclear weapon. One is that the genie is out of the bottle and cannot be put back. Nuclear weapons can, of course, not be disinvented, but this does not mean that we have to keep them in perpetuity. It is a hallmark of a civilized society that it can control—by national legislation or international treaties—the undesirable products of science and technology.

It is on these grounds that biological weapons have been banned, and a similar ban on chemical weapons has now been agree to; the Chemical Weapons Convention has been signed by 156 States and comes into force in 1995.

Another argument is that nuclear weapons have kept the peace in Europe since 1945. This is a supposition without proof, but has gained credence only by constant repetition. It ignores 125 wars, with over 40 million deaths, in other continents; in Europe too we now have a bloody war. It also ignores the fact that during the past four decades there has been a relentless arms race that has resulted in obscenely huge nuclear arsenals. A more serious objection is that a treaty to eliminate nuclear weapons could be violated by a state concealing a clandestine nuclear cache, or by a later 'break-out'. Considering the enormous destructive potential of these weapons, such action might give the transgressing state vast power. However, this is not an insurmountable obstacle.

Even with the present state of technology, it is possible to design a system of verification that will greatly reduce the chances of undetected violation. This technological verification can be enhanced by 'societal verification', that is by calling on the whole community, to report to an international authority any attempted violation of an international treaty. To be effective, this would require a clause in the treaty, and indeed in national legislation, to make such reporting a citizen's duty.

A recent Pugwash study of such schemes, as well as of methods of enforcing treaties in a nuclear-weapon-free world, concluded that the problems of ensuring the integrity of a treaty of eliminate nuclear weapons is less difficult than is generally believed. The study has shown that more international intervention will be needed, such as control of all fissionable material and enforced legislation such as guaranteed protection of whistle-blowing. Measures like these will be constitute infringements on national sovereignty, by limitations of sovereignty will have to be accepted in any case. We live in an ever more interdependent world, and the time has come for an extension of the loyalty to one's nation to a new loyalty, a loyalty to mankind.

Mikhail Gorbachev whose adoption of a new way of thinking has transformed the world, was the first contemporary world leader to realize that a nuclear-weapon-free world is an integral part of stable peace. He suggested the year 2000 as a target date, but this has to be understood to mean the time for agreement on a treaty, rather than for the actual destruction of the weapons, that will take many years.

The main task for the remaining years of this century is to convince world leaders, and the general public, of the necessity of a treaty to eliminate nuclear weapons, binding all nations. During this period we should also seek the implementation of intermediate steps, such as a comprehensive test-ban; adoption of the no-first-use policy; tightening of the safe-guard of the International Atomic Energy Agency; and strengthening the peace-keeping and peace-enforcing powers of the United Nations. An accelerated programme of dismantlement of nuclear warheads, and further deep reductions of nuclear arsenals are of course essential steps.

The very first resolution of the UN General Assembly unanimously called for the elimination of atomic weapons. At long last, the UN is in a position to fulfil the functions for which it has been set up, and the time has come to implement its first resolution; the time has come for a decision to create a nuclear-weapon-free world.

6

Nuclear Arms Race on the Subcontinent

For peace lovers it was a strange and bewildering sight: people dancing and cheering in the streets of New Delhi and Islamabad because their governments had exploded an atomic bomb, politicians bragging about the nuclear capabilities of their countries, the press going wild over the achievements of their scientific institutions. Achievements? In Europe, people had lived for decades under the threat of a nuclear holocaust, they had danced and cheered when the Cold War ended. Now another threat of nuclear war, this time between two of the most populous, but also the most impoverished nations of the world? How could anybody be happy about the news of the successful nuclear tests? Wasn't it absurd that the masses were cheering when their governments were spending the little money they had on the military and on expensive atmomic gadgets instead of combatting poverty in their countries?

The political reactions were quick to follow. A day after India had exploded its first bombs under the Rajasthan desert. In a concerted action, the EU and the G-7 countries as well as the World Bank suspended all new loans for the country. Pakistan met the same fate after it conducted its own atomic test series a few days later. Development cooperation with the two countries has thus been dealt a severe blow. In the last 50 years, both states have been important recipients of World aid.

The worldwide protests and the suspension of development cooperation with India and Pakistan because of the atomic tests may be interpreted as another example of Western hypocrisy. People remember that not long ago, the French government was the target of world-wide indignation because of their series of underground nuclear tests in New Caledonia. Stubbornly, the French President at the time rejected all criticism with the argument that the tests were necessary for the security of France and that tests would end as soon as enough scientific data had been collected. The Chinese similarly displayed total indifference to world opinion when they followed with their own nuclear test series. Not without justice, the Indian and Pakistani governments point out that they have not signed the Nuclear Non-Proliferation Treaty and the Test Ban Treaty and are, therefore, not bound by any international commitment to observe nuclear abstention. India and Pakistan can also rightly point out that the nuclear powers have not fulfilled their own commitments for nuclear disarmament which are part of the Non-Proliferation Treaty. It is really difficult to explain why the five members of the exclusive nuclear club should have the sole right to nuclear arms including the right to develop ever more sophisticated and deadly nuclear weapons. Nobody can be surprised that big countries like India are demanding equality with the nuclear 'haves', and that a hostile neighbour like Pakistan which sees itself as the rival of India on the Subcontinent is trying to stay in the race by building its own bomb.

This is the political side of the coin. The quest of governments to 'keep up with the Joneses', their claim not to be a second class power. But there is also the other side of the coin: Is nuclear equality really in the interest of the people (even if they are dancing in the street when the bomb goes off)? What do they gain from it—for their daily lives, their health, their education, the future of their children? Do their lives not become more insecure, threatened by nuclear war or nuclear accidents? The people in India and Pakistan must answer these questions for themselves. At the moment, gripped by chauvinistic excitement, a majority seems to believe that national aggrandisement is more important for them than better schools, hospitals, houses or roads.

If Indian and Pakistani scientists are able to build nuclear bombs, are they not also able to solve other technical problems in their countries? If their governments have the money for nuclear armaments, should they not be expected to also pay for infrastructure projects, for the provision of fresh water and electricity, for the running of health and education services? How can foreign donors be asked to deal with poverty reduction in the slums or rural areas of their countries, while the military claim a rising share of the national wealth for their ambitious armament programmes?

Certainly, India and Pakistan are sovereign nations and as such they have the same right as the established nuclear powers to spend their money on the atomic bomb. But if they choose that option, they should not ask other countries to help them in their social and economic development. Development cooperation already suffers from a waning acceptance among the population of donor countries. The Indian and Pakistani bombs have given 'development fatigue' another push. People should know this when they rejoice over the arrival of their countries in the nuclear club.

7

The Fabric of Peace

In a world pervaded with violence, the struggle for peace must begin in everyday life. From time immemorial, peace—in the sense of peace between nations and peace within societies—has been exclusively based on the interplay between justice and force, a relationship which is at once conflictual and consensual.

History shows that peace has been and continues to be primarily an affair of state and of states, based on the use of force—in other words, ultimately, on recourse to war. This force is legitimized by highly diverse and in some cases contradictory concepts of justice.

In our time, however, the nature of war has changed. Most often it is no longer waged between states but within their borders. Conflicts within states have become so widespread that warfare has never been so rife—and in many cases so unnoticed—as it is today. Furthermore, violence exists in all our societies in one form or another, even if it does not necessarily erupt into armed confrontation. It takes many forms, and may even been considered the norm. Its most glaring symptom is the growth of inequalities and the social exclusion to which this gives rise. Societies torn to the point of disintegration by civil war or violence are societies whose regulatory mechanisms—the bodies which exist to settle conflicts—are wrapped or paralyzed.

Some might say that this gloomy analysis heralds a future in which war and violence will inevitably prevail. The fact is, however, that these three developments—the changing nature of war, the proliferation of different forms of violence and the weakening of mediatory mechanisms, a process accelerated by globalization and the information revolution—create a new arena in which a culture of peace can emerge. And the prime-mover in this culture of peace will no longer be the state but the individual, in other words each and every one of us.

For surely the road to peace must start within ourselves—in values, behaviour and attitudes which can foster a sense of community that is today threatened. Where else can the foundations of peace be built but in our daily lives, through willingness to listen and talk things through with others on equal terms within the framework of a caring society?

The only obstacles to this enterprise are those we create ourselves, because of ignorance or fanaticism or because of the selfishness that today we are all too often asked to regard as the hallmark of human identity. This approach requires more than good intensions or the occasional act of generosity. The capacity to talk and listen to others and be receptive to their needs can pave the way to peace through an acceptance of a shared responsibility towards other people as well as towards ourselves. The mainspring of the culture of peace is making common cause with others in peace-building projects in everyday life, in whatever area of society we may be involved.

A Participatory Process

This message is not new. The culture of peace is a fabric that has been woven for generations in all societies, though its practices are not necessarily dominated by that specific title. In some places it may be known as tolerance, non-violence or justice. In others, as harmony, solidarity or conviviality. All over the world it has its defenders, some working in obscurity, others in the spotlight of public life. But its scope would be much smaller today had it not been given expression in the disinterested acts of thousands of anonymous men and women capable of listening to others, talking to them and acting with them and on their behalf.

The concept of 'a culture of peace' has clearly not appeared from nowhere. But to have a single expression to describe a multigrade of ethical and practical initiatives may help to highlight their common purpose, make them more widely known and bring them together. It may sharpen the impact and focus of movements that are active in a vast range of fields and settings.

The importance of the culture of peace has now been recognized by the world community. The General Assembly of the United Nations unanimously proclaimed the year 2000 as the International Year for the Culture of Peace. In taking this step, UN Member States accept their own limitations and their urgent need for concept of peace that will be a participatory process to which all members of society can contribute no matter how humble their circumstances.

The culture of peace is intended to be a rallying point that transcends the treaties and agreements that have so often been given short shrift by history. It will become a real and living culture if we take its tenets to heart and shape a common future in our words and deeds.

Peace based exclusively upon the political and economic arrangements of governments would not be a peace which could secure in the unanimous, lasting and sincere support of the peoples of the world, and that the peace must therefore be founded, if it is not to fail, upon the intellectual and moral solidarity of mankind.

8

The End of the Old Order—No Guarantee for Peace and Prosperity

In the last few years, the world has witnessed the collapse of communism and the end of many authoritarian regimes around the globe. In Eastern Europe and the former Soviet Union, multiparty systems with free elections have been introduced. In Afghanistan and Cambodia, Ethiopia and Angola, Nicaragua and Peru leftist governments of various shades have given way to more pluralistic forms of government or are in the process of doing so. In South Africa, the white minority has accepted the black majority rule. All over the world, the old order which was established after World War II is breaking down. Freedom, democracy, self-determination and economic prosperity are the slogans of the revolutions which have swept the repressive regimes away.

But after the initial euphoria over the unexpected successes of the democracy movements, the world is not waking up to the sobering recognition that freedom does not automatically lead to peace and economic progress. In fact, in many countries which have managed to throw off the communist yoke ethnic rivalries have been sharpened by the call for self-determination. Age-old historical animosities between various nationalities and religious groups have come to the fore and are threatening to undo whatever gains have been achieved by introducing a pluralistic system of government.

The former Yugoslavia is a case in point. The state was an artificial creation born after the First World War and the demise of the Austrian—Hungarian and Ottoman Empires. Similar to many of the artificial states in post-colonial Africa, Yugoslavia consisted of a diverse mixture of ethnic and religious nationalities held together primarily by the Charisma of former President Marshal Tito and the Socialist ideology he imposed on the country. The wind of democratic change which blew across the European continent in the wake of Gorbachev's perestroyka also meant for Yugoslavia and hence it is divided between different ethnic or religious groupings.

What has happened in Yugoslavia is also taking place, although to a lesser extent, in Georgia, Armenia, Azerbeidjan, and Moldova where different nationalities have taken arms against each other to fight for their right of self-determination. In Ethiopia, the right to secession has been conceded to the Eritreans by the new democratic government, but already the Oromos and other ethnic groups are threatening to break away from the common state. In Afghanistan, the defeat of the communist regime has not brought peace to the country but the danger of a prolonged bloody civil war between the victorious guerrilla factions. Even in South Africa the end of apartheid marred by intensified inter-ethnic fighting between different African parties and groups.

The conclusion to be drawn from this review of recent developments around the world is certainly not that the call for freedom and democracy will inevitably lead to chaos. However, these developments must warn us that the wonderful concepts of Western philosophical thought will only work in practice if they are accompanied by the necessary spirit of compromise. Democracy functions well in societies which are very homogenous like many of the Western European ones. Even there the system may fail when faced with deeprooted antagonisms as the case of Northern Ireland shows. But in countries which are divided by nationality, race, or religion freedom, democracy, and the right to self-determination may lead to even sharper conflict unless there is a genuine give-

and-take between groups which grants every individual and every group the right to develop according to their own ideas. The older order is breaking down. The communist regimes have collapsed, most of the military dictatorships are on their way out. But in many parts of the world it is not yet clear what will come in their place. One thing is certain: there is no easy way to peace and economic prosperity. The new systems that emerge will have to guarantee the rule of law and the protection of human rights. And they must try to instill a spirit of common values which bridges the cleavages which separate ethnic and religious groups. The oppressive regimes which held together their populations by force must be replaced by governments which have learned the art of compromise—which is the essence of pluralism and democracy.

9

Peace and Poverty

Peace should not be understood in military terms, like absence of armed conflicts. Peace should be understood in a human way in abroad social, political and economic way. Peace should mean social justice between nations and within nations. It should mean establishment of human rights for all people.

In the new context the concept of 'peace' would be the existence of a political and economic environment where each individual human beings is truly free; free from the control of any powerful person or any powerful nation, free from poverty, hunger and indignities, each individual human being free to explore the limits of one's own potential.

Today peace is threatened, more than anything else, by poverty, unjust social and economic order, absence of democracy and environmental degradation.

The cold war could has gone. You can feel the breath of fresh air around the world. Now there is no visible competitor left for capitalism. It is quite risky to live with a philosophy which has no challenger. To be safe, we must go to the essence of the philosophy of capitalism rather than be satisfied with the practices which emerged over years through patchworks of expediency.

Contrary to common belief, it is not the 'free enterprise' which is the essence of capitalism. It is the freedom of individual thought and freedom of individual action which is the essence of capitalism. It is these freedoms which support free enterprise, free trade, free circulation of capital, and free circulation of people.

We must work out a new system, appropriate for the new world, from the basics of capitalism, not from the practices of capitalism. Many of these practices take away freedom, rather than guarantee it. Traps must go. People cannot remain trapped in places where they cannot live because of ecological, political, or economic reasons.

This planet belongs to all people. If some people are trapped somewhere, we must all come forward to remove the causes of their discomfort. At the same time we must leave our shores open for anybody who decides to join us, or any body who decides to part our company.

Poverty denies a person control over his destiny. Poverty means not being able to tell what tomorrow would be like. If we examine the situation carefully we'll see that the poverty is neither created by the poor, nor sustained by the poor. It is the system of policies and institutions that we have built around us that creates and sustains poverty. Poverty is the denial of human rights. Over one billion people live below the absolute poverty line right now on this planet, are denied of almost all human rights. There is no way one can defend the existence of poverty anywhere. Poverty is a disgrace of the entire man-kind. Because we allow another human being to die of hunger, or malnutrition, or common curable diseases, or exposure to climate, we are reduced to less human beings. If a particular world system is responsible for creating this massive poverty we must act to replace it.

Resource-wise or technology-wise, there is no reason why poverty should exist and continue to deepen and widen. If we make up our minds to wipe out poverty from the surface of the earth, the worst aspect of poverty can be removed within the next couple of decades.

We can build a poverty-free world at a fraction of the cost of what we spend on war preparations. Nations become very generous when it comes to making their war-machine heftier in the name of ensuring 'peace'. Can we persuade ourselves to allocate a part of our time, money and intellect to achieve peace by making the people at the bottom the winners, rather than nations winning wars? 'Peace' achieved by winning wars is earned by destroying people. The real peace can be achieved by building people, by reinforcing people, by helping people to reach their potential. Removing poverty is the process of building people.

Each human being is a wonderful creation of the Creator. Each human being is born with great potentials. Poverty denies any opportunity for a person to achieve any of his/her potential. We have built a world system which is in the habit of pushing people down, not building them up. It creates barriers around individuals, rather than remove them.

The most effective step that we must take to remove poverty is to create a system which creates enabling conditions for people and removes the existing barriers. The institutional barriers were skillfully crafted over the centuries to benefit a handful of people.

Resource-poor nations with high incidence of poverty waste away enormous human capability each day by denying poor people the use of their energy and ingenuity. If they could have been made economically active, not only they could have contributed in the national production, they would have helped expand the domestic market for the products produced. The poor can be transformed into the engine of growth if we only allow them to unleash their capacity.

We cannot be at peace with ourselves if we know there is a human being who lives a life worse than an animal. A human being is supposed to live differently than an animal. He/she is supposed to live a life with human dignity. Human dignity is what distinguishes a human being from an animal. When we cannot ensure this dignity for others, our own dignity becomes an empty pretence.

There must be a thousand and one ways to remove poverty from the earth. We may or may not know some of those ways already. Obviously there are many more ways yet to be designed, each more effectively than others. When we shall find them, how many of them we shall find, how quickly we find them, will depend on how eager we are to find them. But to say that poverty cannot be overcome, directly and quickly, is to underestimate the capacity of human mind.

Poverty is homogeneous only when considered from the point of view of income or consumption: the uniformity of the poor as a category exists only on the level of the fact that they have little to consume. When considered from the point of view of production, *i.e.*, the circumstances in which the poor must operate to gain their income, the conditions of poverty are extraordinary diverse. A concrete grasp of these diverse circumstances is the first step in developing relevant instruments to address not only the problems of the poor, but also the challenge of taking advantage of the opportunities available to them.

The conventional means of measuring economic progress, such as Gross National Product per capita, tell us little about the real nature of poverty. In recent years this sort of yardstick has been supplemented by measurements of food security, income distribution, and social development (encompassing health and education). These offer the possibility of composite indices, allowing the development of more rounded characterizations and comparisons of poverty at the national level. However, these principally refer to the symptoms of poverty, not to the relational factors generating it. Poverty is not a state of being, it is the effect of dynamic processes. While it is important to know where poverty is greatest, it is critical to know why it exists. This inquiry necessarily leads away from the nature of the poor as individuals to the nature of their social and physical environment.

Poverty is not only a personal phenomenon, it is a social status. As such, while its effects can be measured on the level of the individual, its causes must be sought elsewhere. From the point of view of poverty alleviation the process of becoming is just as important as the state of being.

At the heart of poverty is the inadequate access of the poor to productive resources. Low incomes tend to reflect inadequate means of production, not incompetent producers. However, poverty in India is not simply a reflection of private resources. A broad range of 'external' factors impinge on incomes, among them the following:

National Policies

One of the ironies of Indian development is that while no government wants poverty, many policies contribute to it—what is given in anti-poverty programmes is drained away by other policies. The poor do not always come out ahead in the balance—they are often net 'donors' to the rest of society. Frequent reference is made to unsustainable forms of development—to urban over-expansion, industrialization based on subsidies, and to public sector engorgement. What is less frequently realized is that the bill for these phenomena is often presented to the rural poor. Taxation of exports to sustain sectors with little export potential of their own and subsidized food imports to supply the urban population are policies that are often paid for by the rural poor. In many areas of India, exports are agricultural goods produced by small farmers. Here export taxes contribute to rural poverty. The same is true of 'cheap' food imports which depress the prices paid to small farmers for their food crops.

'Structural imbalance' is not only a recipe for increasing external indebtedness, it is also a recipe for increasing the poverty of the rural population. The political weakness of the poor in most areas is not only the basis for inadequate poverty alleviation programmes and policies—it is the basis for an actual transfer of their income to more socially influential groups. While it is often correctly asserted that the poor are the first to suffer from adjustments involving public social expenditure cuts, it is often the case that they also have the most to gain from the elimination of policy-based economic distortions that reflect social power rather than productive efficiency and potential.

Demographic Factors

Accelerated population growth is a long-term contributor to poverty. In India the incomes of the poor have declined, mortality rates are also falling, pushing the numbers up. In the meantime, land is becoming scarcer, plots more fragmented and the soil and pasture increasingly degraded. This phenomenon is not without its policy dimensions. As long as the poor remain undercapitalized, and essential determinant of household income is the amount of labour available to it household economic strategies favour large families. While population policy has a role to play, possibly more critical is a change in the economic environment. Access to capital and more secure income changes perceptions of the need for labour. In the medium—and long-term, population dynamics are driven by the underlying productive systems. As long as the production systems of the poor remain underdeveloped, population growth remains high, restricting even the future possibility of development.

Natural Resource Management and the Environment

If poverty is both cause and effect of rapid population expansion, so poverty is both cause and effect of many dimensions of degradation of the environment. Many of the rural poor, but by no means all, live in areas of extreme environment fragility, a circumstance often prompted by high level of control by the better-off over more stable and productive resource areas. Here the poor are extraordinarily exposed to the dangers of erosion, whittling away at an already meager productive base. The threat is not entirely due to nature. Rather, poverty accelerates erosion. Without capital, the poor are frequently unable to invest in even traditional methods of soil and water conservation. And without sufficient land they are forced to shorten fallow periods, putting further strain on the resource base. As in the case of population growth, the result is strain not only on the poor, but on the entire Indian economy. Given the extremely limited economic alternatives, the solution to this problem is not to forbid the use of environmentally fragile resources to the poor, it is to change the conditions under which their use takes places. Access to conservation technology is important; but more so are security of land tenure and resources to invest.

Combating poverty means not only increasing the production of the poor, but also preserving and enhancing the long-term value of the resources they control. What this very often means, in practice is assisting the poor in reestablishing a stable relationship with fragile resource. Prevailing processes in many areas involve the gradual—and sometimes not so gradual—depletion of natural resources, to the detriment of all. Part of the answer to this is conservation. Part of the answer is also to provide viable economic alternatives to the poor, reducing their dependence on erosion-prone crop and livestock practices.

Exploitative Intermediates

The poor are not unaware of the pressure upon them, and also of means of overcoming them. Their ability to respond, however, is severely impaired by social powerlessness. The poor are surrounded by a dense network of public and private factors reducing their freedom of action, and actually draining what few resources they do have. Members of the network include traders and moneylenders capitalizing upon the economic weakness of the poor, and engaging them in unequal exchanges. They also include public agencies either indifferent to the requirement of the socially uninfluential, or actively engaged in extracting 'surplus' for use by other groups. Not to be excluded from this are organisations which are ostensibly 'for' the poor, but which, in fact, serve as systems of containment and control.

10

A Crucial Encounter

Genetic tests and treatments must not be allowed to create new forms of discrimination between those who, for whatever reason, can or want to take advantage of them, and those who cannot, mostly for lack of money. If a scientific discovery can form the basis of a technology, then it is highly probable that the technology will eventually be applied. Today this lesson of history is causing anxiety among politicians, scientists and public opinion concerned about the current far-reaching developments in biotechnologies.

It is now possible to penetrate to the very essence of living things as a result of spectacular scientific advances that are gradually revealing the innermost mechanisms of life. The technologies based on this field of knowledge offer humanity for the first time astonishing powers to revolutionize the process of creating and developing human beings and, ultimately, the human species. Technically speaking, these breakthroughs could lead to the revival, in even more effective guises, of eugenic practices we hoped had been buried forever. Fortunately, this nightmare scenario seems highly unlikely.

But history also shows that new technologies are rarely applied without a framework of rules and procedures designed to ensure that they are beneficially used. Human progress has always been driven by the winds of freedom, including freedom of enquiry and initiative, but human beings have always tried to head in the right direction and to respect certain limits. The biologists have done their work: they have sown the seeds of vast possibilities. Now it is up to society to make sure that only the benefits are harvested. The biotechnology revolutions beckons humanity to a crucial encounter between science and ethics.

Where human reproduction is concerned, as with technology in general, we must be guided by respect for three basic and interdependent principles dignity, freedom and solidarity.

For human dignity to be respected, each person must be regarded as unique. This position has far-reaching consequences for human procreation. First of all, it rules out cloning as a means of reproduction because this technique, which is almost upon us, involves genetically 'duplicating' an existing person. More generally, predetermining the basic characteristics of a future person, notably trying to enhance their future physical or mental capacities, violates the very essence of human individuality. This kind of engineering would end up by depriving individuals of that which is theirs alone—the mysterious processes whereby their unique genetic heritage emerges and interacts in its own unique way with their environment.

Advances in prenatal scanning and testing techniques may confront parents with grave new decisions. The danger is that various kinds of pressures or even regulations will develop which only allow 'genetically correct' people to be born. This would be totally unacceptable. No authority—be it political, social or economic—should be able to enact such a 'genetic order', still less impose it.

So increasing emphasis must be laid on solidarity. Genetic tests and treatments must not be allowed to create new forms of discrimination between those who, for whatever reason, can or want to take advantage of them, and those who cannot mostly for lack of money.

The risk of uncontrolled, unmonitored genetic engineering increasingly looms over us. But we are starting to see the emergence of a new 'responsible' form of genetic engineering in which the power of science is subjected to the power of ethics an ethics that benefits everyone, not just a few, and looks towards future generations, not just short-term interests.

11

A Universal Responsibility

Each of us is responsible for replacing the logic of force with the logic of reason and respect for the view of others. On the threshold of a new millennium, the issue of responsibility is taking on a new dimension. Humankind is still beset by war and violence. It also faces new global challenges. The impact of human activity on our planet is so great that for the first time in recorded history, we may be approaching the point of no return. The widening asymmetry within and between countries, environmental destruction and flourishing arms sales raise doubts about many of civilization's values and standards. How can we handle new global threats? History shows that no situation is hopeless if risks are identified early enough.

The conflicts that have arisen since the end of the Cold War have erupted not as a consequence of new freedoms but in reaction to earlier oppression or repression. Suspicion, intolerance and hatred built up over decades, even centuries. But alongside the armed strife of recent years, humankind has begun to demonstrate a new skill in resolving conflicts. Mozambique, El Salvador, the Philippines the changes in South Africa that would have been inconceivable just a few years ago, the efforts for peace in the Middle East and finally, the beginning of a settlement in Northern Ireland are all examples proving that conflict is not inevitable. They demonstrate that breakthroughs to peace can be made by dialogue, mediation, negotiation and imagination not force.

That is why the transition from a culture of war to a culture of peace is the foremost challenge as the twentieth century draws to a close. To succeed we—all of us, day in and day-out must not only do away with approaches based on force and imposition, but profoundly change cultural attitudes and daily behaviour.

We must use imagination and resolution to go to the roots of world problems and nip conflicts in the bud or, better still, prevent them. Learning to live together means daring to share, daring to do things differently, and daring to dream of a better, safer more just and human world. It also means having the resolve and courage to transform our dreams into reality.

Here I wish to underline the pivotal role of education in promoting a culture of peace. By education, I mean not only formal instruction in schools but also informal training within a whole range of cultural institutions, including in the very first place the family and the media.

Who will be responsible for changing the culture of war into a cultural of peace? Governments, parliaments, intergovernmental organisations, we might reply. The answer is correct, but it is not the only one. The transformation cannot be achieved without the active involvement of those with financial resources and influence. This answer would also be true, though only partly so. For in the final analysis, replacing the logic of force and confrontation with the logic of reason and respect for the views of others is a responsibility that belongs to all nations and all citizens, to each of us no matter how great or small the scope of our individual responsibility. The challenge of promoting a culture of peace is so broad and far-reaching that it can only be accomplished if it becomes a priority for the entire United Nations system. The dream of achieving a world without strife and violence is urgent.

The Mahatma Gandhi said, "In the midst of darkness, light prevails." It is that light which is spread by the democratic values enshrined in our constitution: justice, freedom, equality and solidarity.

12

Science to What Purpose

Are the welfare and interest of the public being served by the priorities of researchers, the thrust of their work, the ways in which they are organised, the funding they receive, and the circulation of their findings?

Science reigns triumphant. Never has it been so powerful and influential. It has conquered diseases which have decimated whole populations. It has abolished exhausting physical labour and wearisome repetitive tasks. It has vanquished distance and pushed back the frontiers of our knowledge of the infinitely large and the infinitely small, in both the inanimate and the living world.

In short, it has acquired the ability to shape our lives, to change life itself. But it has also increased its capacity to destroy life. The strength of an army can rest on the number and determination of its combatants but it is also, and chiefly, based on the technological sophistication of their weaponry. The bombing of Iraq, and now of Serbia, are the latest examples.

Yet science is wavering. For the first time since the Enlightenment, the way science can be used is being challenged. The link between scientific progress and social progress is weakening and signs of obscurantism are appearing. Hiroshima sounded the alarm. Then the crisis of the environment, triggered by the dominant mode of development, turned questioning of science into a worldwide issue. This form of development is inseparable from a frantic and indiscriminate quest for technological innovation. Finally, advances in biotechnology, which harbour many grave dangers from human dignity, are often too closely bound up with the selfish interests of their promoters.

No one blames science for not knowing everything. No one criticizes it because it has not yet found a vaccine against AIDS or reached a conclusion about the theory of the Big Bang. It has never been claimed of science, as it has of history, that it has come to an end. It must keep on tirelessly probing the enduring mysteries of life.

But science can no longer avoid—and nor can we—the basic question of what and who it is for. In other words, are the welfare and interests of the public being served by the priorities of researchers, the thrust of their work, the ways in which they are organised, the funding they receive, and the circulation of their findings? Or are scientists looking mainly in the direction of high-spending consumers at the expense of long-term basic research? Because of the growing 'privatization' of research, are we not tending to overlook essential and universal human needs which cannot immediately be met?

Those who are excluded from this new 'scientific power' must make their voices heard. For example, the inhabitants of the 600,000 villages which have no electricity or the world's two billion people without access to drinking water have the right to ask science to find solutions adapted to their very meagre resources. Humanity also has the right to ask science to give priority to research into processes of global disruption and ways of coping with them. What's more, all citizens have the right to ask science to further our understanding of the mechanisms of inequality and exclusion which are gradually undermining peace and democracy.

One major purpose of this paper will be to see that the benefits of science go primarily to all those who have hitherto been unreached. Their conditions will only improve if they have access to the mighty power of science.

13

Social Summit

The issues which the World Summit for Social Development is called upon the tackle—poverty, unemployment and social exclusion—are among the most critical of our time. In spite of the considerable material gains that have been registered during the past 50 years, in spite of the tremendous technological progress that has been achieved, in spite of the more favourable international political climate resulting from the end of the Cold War, poverty continues to grow and inequalities continue to widen.

Over a billion people are living in poverty. Some 30 per cent of the world's labour force is not productively employed. Many societies are being torn apart by racial, ethnic and religious conflict and intolerance. These social issues constitute the greatest threat to peace, stability and prosperity in today's world and need to be tackled with urgency and determination by policy-makers at the highest level.

If the Social Summit is to leave its mark on history, it will have to be more than a ritual gathering of Heads of State and Government. It will have to result in a perceptible improvement in the social situation in countries throughout the world—in the short and medium term, not in some indefinite future.

It will have to acknowledge that these are truly global problems which require global action in a world characterized by growing inter-dependence. National action, important though it is, will no longer suffice.

A collective commitment by all the nations of the world to the goal of full, productive and freely chosen employment is of crucial importance to the work of the Summit. It is only through their labour that individuals can contribute to the creation of wealth for their benefit and for society as a whole, can lift themselves out of poverty, can be integrated into social, economic, political and cultural life.

In view of the growing globalization of the economy—characterized by freer trade and capital movements and greater exposure to world market forces—no country acting alone can achieve full employment without a favourable international economic environment. But we also expect emphasis to be laid on appropriate national strategies: macro-economic policies, industrial and agricultural policies which favour the growth of job-creating, enterprises, education and training policies, active labour market policies which enable individuals and enterprises to adjust rapidly to changing market conditions, and policies which grant all citizens equal access to employment, education and training.

We expect the Summit to commit all nations to take special action to improve the employment prospects of those who are in a particularly disadvantaged position in the labour market—young people, disabled people, ethnic minorities. We expect it to recognize the special contribution made by women to the general welfare—through their role in the family and in production—and to end the pervasive discrimination and inequality still suffered by women.

We expect the Summit to emphasize that full employment does not mean the creation of any sort of jobs, but of high-quality jobs. We expect it to recognize the basic rights of workers—freedom of association and collective bargaining, freedom from forced labour, equal pay for work of equal value, equality of opportunity in employment and occupation.

We expect it to recognize the importance of measures which provide social security and minimum wages, which protect against arbitrary dismissal and which ensure occupational safety and health.

However balance has to be struck between the need for adequate protection and incomes on the one hand and need not to price workers and enterprises out of the market on the other. Realistic and socially acceptable solutions can only be found if those most directly concerned—employers and workers—are fully involved in decision-making on these matters through organisations of their own choosing.

Finally, and perhaps most important of all, we expect the Summit to determine the institutional framework and mechanisms for following up its conclusions. Their is no point in adopting fine-sounding commitments and policies if there is no means of ensuring and monitoring follow-up action.

If the Summit fails to establish such a framework, its conclusions could well prove to be a hollow text that will quickly be forgotten.

14

Rural Poverty in India and Development as a Policy Challenge

Poverty can be overcome, and that the poor can increase their income and production within an appropriate framework. Part of that framework is made up of a flow of resources and local-level institutional development, and there is considerable scope for improvement in both. However, the impact of investment and organisation is strictly determined by the nature of the policy environment. While project and programmes can bring some relief to the rural poor, substantial change needs a strong policy commitment. While the poor can overcome poverty, they will not be able to until this becomes a major focus of national policy and action. In the main, this sort of commitment has not been made in the past—at the expense of both the poor and overall development in many areas.

The current state of India is highly contradictory. On the one hand, there is proclamation of a new order; on the other, increasing value is given to sectional and short-term national and group interests. With an overt concern with the India's poor goes an equal weight given to concern with economic mechanisms and relations that pay little attention to poverty and foster more inequality. The dangers of this situation are real. The lack of concrete attention being given to change will mean greater economic polarization. Greater polarization among the better-off, and between the better-off and the poor—means instability and lack of consensus, a lack of legitimacy.

Poverty is far-reaching, and ought to be curtailed. In a period in which resources everywhere appear restricted, this seems not to be an attractive proposition at the practical level. Welfare is everywhere giving way to production as an imperative, just as public expenditure is giving way to private accumulation. Poverty alleviation does not appear to be an idea whose time has come. The objections are great, but they are also misplaced. Poverty alleviation is not necessarily a drain upon accumulation, and it is not primarily a public activity. Poverty alleviation is primarily the activity of the poor themselves, and their progress necessarily involves productive expansion. If this potential for private expansion has not been realized, it is not because of the nature of the poor, it is because of the way in which national economic affairs have been organised. Economic policy has been oriented towards the better-off—not infrequently at the expense of the poor. Given the historic association between wealth and power, the definition of development in terms of the large and the wealthy is hardly surprising.

There is the possibility of associated growth involving both large-scale and small-scale production, the better-off and the poor. The realization of this possibility might result from a new social compact. This social compact is not a commitment to social safety nets and welfare, both of which seem to presuppose that the poor are somehow necessarily out of the growth field. It is a commitment to abolishing artificial and onerous terms of exchange that discriminate against the poor, to investing resources where there are real opportunities for gain, irrespective of whether the economic agents concerned and rich or poor, and to creating the space for the poor to organise to pursue their social and economic interests.

There is a need for a new growth model consistent with new social realities. While the 1980s was a period of clearing away many of the obstacles to development, it was not a period in which there emerged a clear vision of what represented the positive basis for growth, beyond, that is, a general prescription of market-driven operations. The model must pass from admonition to positive prescription to fuel growth by integrating the poor in their rightful place in the production function. It must redefine the position of public expenditure in the development process, and seek to establish market structures which are both equitable and open to the participation of the economically weaker elements of the population. Most of all it must revalue the position and contribution of the poor and small-scale producers in the growth process, particularly in the agricultural sector, but no exclusively agriculture.

This means that the issue is not so much one of less government, but of government, both national and local, finding a new rationale for action, including, *inter alia*, creating conditions that will effectively unleash the productive potential of the rural poor.

Financial flows to the poorest Indians are not likely to undergo a very major expansion, especially through private channels. Development will rely very much on the mobilization of their own resources, and many of these resources are in the hands of the poor, are, indeed, not only the human capital embodied in the poor but also their assets which, while small, individually are cumulatively important in India. The growth model for the 1990s will have to embrace that fact, and build upon it. The paradox of most development models is that they have emphasized the value of what Indians do not have, while devaluing what they have: capital intensity has been promoted in situations of scarcity of capital, at the expense of abundant labour and of low-cost methods of manifold increase of the productivity of assets of which the poor do dispose. In a not very indirect way, the creation of poverty has been subsidized. Poverty alleviation is neither a special topic nor a low-cost substitute for growth. It is neither more nor less 'social' than development in general. It is part of the formulation of any sustainable strategy of economic development. In the 1990s it may, and perhaps should, become the dominant issue—not as an alternative to the structural reorganisations of the 1980s, but as a means of filling a growth framework with substance.

15

Democracy and the Market Economy

Today the idea of democracy is triumphant; the model is in principle embraced in most countries the world over. You may say that the very word democracy has been hailed and misused earlier in history. The most repressing and totalitarian regimes have tried to mask themselves as 'real' or 'peoples' democracies. What has happened, however, is a historical demasking of these false pretences.

What exactly do we mean by democracy? There is now a general agreement that democracy cannot be defined by purpose or policy or levels of mass mobilisation. It must be defined as a political system where different parties or individuals compete for power through regular free elections where all adult citizens have a vote. Moreover, a democracy must uphold certain basic human rights and well-defined freedoms which make the political process possible, and respect the opinion and integrity of the individual. No other definitions hold, and we should be careful when we talk about 'real' democracy versus 'formal' democracy. A society which is real life upholds the constitutional or formal democratic principles and which in practice applies the rights these principles imply, is by definition a democracy. A society with a beautiful-sounding constitution but where none or few of these rights are respected is certainly not a democracy.

Democratic Government no Guarantee for Equality

It is important to understand that democratic government does not necessarily mean good government in the sense that those in power make wise well-considered decisions. Nor does it mean that conflicts inherent in the society are reduced to a minimum. Demands for democracy, social justice and a better life have historically gone hand in hand, but this does not mean that the establishment of a democratic system actually does lead to an improvement in social conditions or equality. It is also quite clear that some societies have a sort of outer shell of democracy but in reality, exclude large groups of people from having any political influence whatsoever. The actual differences in living conditions are so enormous and so entrenched that these people have no confidence at all in the political system even if it is democratic according to the definition. In these cases—for example in some Latin American countries—one can talk of a "masked hegemony with competing elites" where the outcome of struggles for power has little relevance for the masses. It is a sort of social and political half-authoritarian system—but disguised as a democracy—where the military often have a significant influence.

In the rhetoric of the day the terms market economy and democracy are used as if they were synonymous or atleast naturally emerging at the same time. But this is wrong—or atleast misleading. When the market economy or capitalism finally established itself in the 1800s and came to characterize modern industrial civilization, democracy was at best in its infancy. In fact one could argue that democracy grew out of the contradictions and social dynamism inherent in the market economy of the capitalistic system. In this century we have a long list of terrifying and repressive regimes which have nevertheless upheld the virtues of a market economy. That some of these regimes have for ideological and security reason been hailed as bastions against communism, and also dignified members of the so-called free world does not transform them into democracies. In this company it is perhaps unnecessary to remind ourselves that the colonial system was assuredly not democratic, but was certainly based on capitalistic or market economic principles. It is the sad but irrefutable historical coupling between Western democracy, colonialism, and the plundering of resources in the name of the market economy which for understandable reasons meant that many of the leaders of national liberation movements looked for other models for the development of their young nations. In this connection it can be worth remembering what Nelson Mandela said soon after his release from 26 years of prison in the market economic but racist state of South Africa. "When we in ANC during 40 years struggled for democracy we were put in prison by the same people who are now telling us how we should behave to promote the democracy we have been rejected by all these years".

While we can see that a market economy does not automatically lead to democracy, a functioning democracy—as we have defined it—does seem to require some form of free economic system.

Democracy and Economic Freedom

Theoretically, it is conceivable that a political democracy could be combined with an economy totally controlled by the Government—but experience has shown this to be very difficult. One could even argue that it is by definition impossible since democracy implies a certain freedom of economic choice and independent economic actors. A functioning democratic system presupposes what is now often referred to as a civil society—in practice, independent, institutions, companies, organisations, the media etc., regulated by law but not subject to or controlled by those in power.

We must also see clearly that there are no unambiguous relations between economic growth, development and democracy. Democratic governments are neither very successful when it comes to structural reforms which may be to the disadvantage of important interests in the society, nor when it comes to welfare. The developing countries which have achieved the greatest success economically and socially over the last 20 years are the East Asian countries—which all have had various kinds of more or less authoritarian systems.

However, that does not mean that you can use these countries as models for the rest of the world. There is no globally valid link between an authoritarian form of regime and economic development, not even when development is defined only in terms of autocentric growth. Many social scientists—have tried to find some systematic connection between what we call development or modernisation on the one hand, and the political system on the other—but all have failed.

It is also obvious that one of several pre-requisites for economic growth and development is legitimate and reasonably well functioning government and governance. If the free market is to be a motor for development and improved welfare, and not just a meeting place for robber barons, the mafia and speculators, you must have a regulating and supportive state. If economic history teaches us anything, it is just this. Consider the astounding development in Germany after the war, or in Japan and the other East Asian countries some years later. There are many differences, but what they have in common is a well-functioning government apparatus with a long tradition.

Today we find ourselves in a historical situation where a large number of countries in the former communist states of Europe, in Africa, Asia and Latin America are at one and the same time trying to establish a new democratic system and new economic mechanisms. The situation is unique, and the intrinsic problems are unprecedented. Democracy as an idea has triumphed but in its practice it is in profound trouble. It is no exaggeration to talk of the crisis of democracy.

The former communist countries are certainly in crisis. As a by-product of the past regimes, there is an intensive suspicion of the political institutions, of the state and the parties—and in this way also the legitimacy of democracy and the ability of the politicians to deal with the fundamental problems of society has been undermined. The lack of a democratic tradition is not overcome from one day to the next.

Many of the developing countries have similar difficulties. The introduction of a multiparty system does not in itself mean that one can manage the conflicts and social problems in a democratic way.

Countries in Transition

Both in the East and the South countries are trying, at one and the same time, to change the political and economic system. When the whole society is convulsed by economic changes, and where peoples' living conditions fundamentally change, it is not easy to develop and maintain a political system based on compromise and respect, including respect for minorities.

As in previous history the deep crises of legitimacy and general frustration feed national and ethnical conflicts. These conflicts establish themselves in societies where the authoritarian system, economic crises and the break down of traditional values rob people of any kind of kinship other than ethnical.

We cannot avoid seeing disturbing signs of this crisis of democracy also in the so-called 'established democracies' of the rich countries.

It is obvious that the state of democracy varies from country to country, as do the reasons for a feeling of dejection. But there are some similarities too.

The continuing and noticeable internationalisation limits the national freedom of political choices, available alternatives, and makes it more difficult for people to see the connection between 'politics' and their actual living conditions. The governments are restrained by international economic events. The reaction of the stock exchange may be more important than that of the voters. The election results influence the stock exchange prices—but is it perhaps not also so that the stock exchanges, indirectly, also influence the election results? People feel themselves to be the victims of major economic changes, but no one seems to be responsible and they themselves feel they have little chance of influencing the outcomes. The absence of clearly identifiable alternatives between the larger political parties provides opportunities for the populists and the extremists.

There is indeed reason to reflect on the lessons of the history of our turbulent and cruel century.

Priority for Growth

There is today much concern about the lack of resources for such urgent needs as the reconstruction of the East, a concerted attack on poverty and human development in the poorest countries, and environmental investments of all kinds. If the growth of world output returns to the levels of the 1980s, total output would grow by about one trillion dollars a year. There is, infact, no other way to resolve the economic and political crises multiplying in the world community than to give priority to the restoration of growth.

We are certainly not at the end of history as someone has argued. We are rather at a dramatic turning point, a moment of many possibilities and many dangers. What we do now, for a few years ahead, may direct the future for several decades—like the dramatic and fateful years immediately after the second world war. All nations, all governments, have a responsibility. The rich world has a special responsibility, not just moral because of its enormous economic and political power.

16

Corruption

Everyday the community is being stunned as reports of irregular practices compete for press headlines. The impression is that bribery and corruption, in one form or another is both extensive and increasing; although systematic statistics in this area are rare for obvious reasons.

What is corruption? The list of possibilities is extensive. It starts with the outright bribery of government officials and the more ambiguous question of political contributions; then there are a whole range of activities that could be considered to some degree corrupt—covering such things as the misuse of company assets for political favours, kickbacks and protection money for the police, payola to disc jockeys, sympathetic feature articles in return for advertising revenue, free revenue, free junkets for MP's and journalists, secret price-fixing agreements, obtaining parts in films for reasons not wholly related to acting ability, insider dealing of various kinds, as well as the improper use of the 'old boy' network.

All these forms of behaviour have one thing in common. They are attempts to influence the outcome of a decision where the nature of that influence is not made public. Essentially the practices are nothing more or less than the abuse of power.

Reasons for Spread of Corruption

There are several reasons for this spread of corrupt practices. First the concentration of power in larger and larger units; particularly when combined with rapid growth where the channels of accountability are underdeveloped. It is also widespread in 'mature' societies where highly developed networks attempt to preserve the 'status-quo' and further their vested interests.

As Gunnar Myrdal, the renowned economist, succinctly put it in his classical study 'Asia Drama'. "Generally speaking, the habitual practice of bribery and dishonesty tends to pave the way for an authoritarian regime, whose disclosures of corrupt practices in the preceding government and whose punitive action against offenders provide a basis for its initial acceptance by the articulate strata of the population".

While corruption inevitably undermines the political system, or organisational structure, in the long run those involved are invariably more concerned with the short term. Also corrupt practices can be infectious. In certain areas companies with high ethical standards have either been forced out of business, or have had to give up their high standards, where their rivals have been willing to pay bribes to win orders.

It is sometimes claimed that 'first class' companies are relatively "clean-atleast in the narrow sense—because they can afford to be. They are already powerful and influential, with a network of informal contacts and relationships, so they do not need to beg and bribe as a way of getting business. It is often the new company trying to break into a new market, or the company fighting for survival, that is the most likely to use bribes to cut corners. Hence the problem is prevalent both in periods of rapid economic growth and change, as well as in periods of economic crisis; although there is some evidence to suggest that more of it might come to the surface, usually by accident, during the latter than former.

It is also occasionally argued—usually not very convincingly—that corruption does not actually impede development but may even accelerate it by helping to by-pass bureaucratic red-tape. However, life is rarely that simple and entrepreneurs within this approach invariably ensure that all too frequently that payments are made and nothing gets done!

A recipe for disaster especially as it is somewhat difficult for the aggrieved party to complain under these circumstances.

Unfair Distribution of Income

In some cases it has been known for payments to be strictly calculated as a defined percentage of the expected gain from a legislative concession. While on other occasions payments have become so institutionalised that they are virtually another form of taxation. However, the differences between a 'corruption surcharge' and taxation needs to be recognised; the former are rarely made openly, they are usually unfair and rarely are they seen to be fair. In addition they usually redistribute the income in a socially regressive direction.

The important factor appears to be to ensure that, wherever possible, practices and channels of accountability are made public. In practice, there are few absolute principle, and trade-offs are inevitable. The key element is the extent to which any decision is made openly and appears to have wide-spread support. If deals can be kept completely private, the social and political repercussions will, atleast in the short term, be minimal. But anyone working on such an assumption, who then finds his, or her, activities made public, is likely to be in a dangerously exposed position.

In general, companies prefer clear and accepted codes of behaviour—for everyone. But deciding on what is fair competition, as opposed to unfair advantage can be complicated and subjective as both individual and corporate standards of acceptable behaviour are conditioned by the traditions and characteristics of the society in which they operate.

What can be done to eliminate corruption in both its monetary and non-monetary forms? The first step is usually to pass a law making atleast monetary corruption an offence. It is assumed that unaccountable assets are by themselves sufficient evidence of corruption. However, there is little evidence to suggest that the extent of corruption is related to the type of legislation, as the problems of law enforcement are usually formidable in this area.

The paradox at the centre of an anti-corruption programme is that the laws must first be passed by governments and the standards, set by politicians are a vital element in this process, yet these are the very people who are most likely to profit from illicit payments.

Of course no measures against corruption are likely to be effective if officials are so badly paid that they cannot live on their salaries. As a result many have combined an anti-corruption programme with an increase in official salaries. Unfortunately, although poor pay frequently drives people to extort bribes higher pay by itself, rarely stops it. This is partly due to the perennial problem that few people consider themselves adequately paid and partly because in both the corporate and political arenas ineffective control systems provide a fertile breeding-ground for the more blatant forms of monetary corruption. In order to reduce these abuses the role of independent auditors needs to be strengthened in almost every country.

It is not altogether surprising that the normal agencies of law enforcement usually find themselves unable to curb, let alone eliminate, corruption. Because of this governments have set up special bodies charged with the task of investigation and enforcing anti corruption legislation. Although sizable penalties and more independent powers of inquiry are obviously helpful, it is difficult to establish any relationship between the existence of special organisations and the extent of corruption. It does not need emphasising that these agencies invariably run the risk of concentrating on the more blatant forms of monetary occupation and rarely investigate its more subtle forms. Related to this area is the whole subject of establishing a legitimate basis for 'whistleblowing'.

Power and Corruption

Corruption tends to be most frequent where governments take on greater powers to bestow special privileges on various sectors of the economy and society. Where there is this concentration of power there is an urgent need to ensure more open accountability. The media is frequently the key to this process of accountability but, unfortunately, it is often either controlled by the authorities, or subject to its own internal pressures from advertisers or other influences. Corruption is the universal disease of the body politic it varies only in degree and visibility. It is least in extent when the press is free and uncorrupted and when the public are organised sufficiently to demand honest government. It is usually most widespread when the opposite conditions apply. But how often are cases revealed as a result of penetrating investigative journalism, rather than vulture like exposure once the revelation has come to light? And how often do unethical practices come to light from the systematic application of the control machinery, rather than almost by an accident?

Nevertheless, in essence, the problem of corruption is easily solved. If everyone worked on the assumption that whatever they did to influence a decision would be public knowledge, the vast majority of monetary and non-monetary corrupt practices would never arise.

Recent revelations suggest there are signs we are moving away from that utopian state. Yet, if this trend is not controlled and reversed, the consequences for individuals, companies will continue to be extremely serious. It can even lead to a crisis of confidence in the system itself.

For all these reasons it is not surprising to find that ethics is now one of the most rapidly expanding subject areas everywhere.

17

Fighting for Equality on All Fronts

In the wake of unemployment, global competition and deregulation, more and more women are joining an unforgiving job market. Are they in a position to exercise force against the discrimination they experience, and can they impose equality of opportunity? To change things, women need to enter into combat on several fronts.

"For a long time, companies considered publicity to be a luxury and, in difficult times, the 'advertising and communications' budget was always the first to be slashed. Today, employers have become more aware that publicity has become a trump card in their strategy. Why can't a similar awareness become possible on the subject of women's employment?"

Financial problems and an evolution of mentality are the two core themes discussed in this paper on the Equality of Women in the world of work.

A Dual Observation

It is of a two-fold general observation: women are more increasingly joining the ranks of the active population: however, this trend is not matched by a parallel improvement in the quality of jobs to which they have access.

It is foreseen that women's rate of participation will be close to that of men by the year 2010. In developing countries, the rate of women's activity is only 31 per cent on average, but this figure does not take into account the very large female participation in the informal sector and in agriculture. Thus, for example, in India, the adoption of a more general definition of 'economic activity' pushed the participation of women from 13 to 88 per cent.

Women remained constrained in a relatively limited number of 'feminine' sectors and occupations which are generally less well-paid and are less prestigious. During the last decade, however, an upward trend has emerged and more women are acceding to management and administrative posts and to specialized and technical professions. Moreover, an increasing number of women are setting up their own businesses. It can be noted, nonetheless, that very few salaried women are able to reach the higher echelons of responsibility due to the well-known 'glass ceiling'.

Among other disturbing observations is the increase in part-time work, which is especially prevalent among women with young children; other types of atypical work include temporary and occasional jobs, homework and subcontracting. Part-time workers are often young women who are less educated and less qualified than the average, which makes them more vulnerable. In Africa, in Asia and in Latin America, women are being called upon more and more to find work in the informal sector.

Even though some progress has been made in the area of wages, women's salaries are still between one-half and 80 per cent of those earned by men. Women's work is underestimated in most of the societies, and their income does not match their contribution to the economy. The difference in wages cannot be attributed to conditions of work alone. In the United States, in 1994 a woman in her twenties was likely to be earning 90 per cent of the rate of salary of her male counterpart.

Financial Problems

Financial problems and mentality issues emerged as two essential factors at every stage of the analysis of the causes of these persistent differences. The Forum's participants' general consensus was that they should be tackled first of all.

Financial implications cannot be separated from the issue of women's employment, whether it is to justify its need or on the contrary to discourage it, or to explain the absence or lack of training of women who are available in the job market. Some examples are:

- In the countries in transition in Central and Eastern Europe companies under pressure to increase profits do not want to maintain social support services, which earlier had backed women's participation in the active population. These pressures are compelling women to leave the job market as the cost of child care increases.
- In developing countries, especially in Asia, Africa and Latin America, the worsening of poverty and the increase in the number of single-parent families are requiring women in turn towards income-generating activities, but the lack of training and difficult access to credit constitute a major handicap.
- In Thailand, one of the major causes of young village girls resorting to prostitution is the state of poverty of their families, who are unable to afford secondary schooling for them.

Prejudices and Stereotypes

Several examples can also be found in the persisting traditions and stereotypes which are an obstacle in the path of women's march to equality of opportunity in the world of work.

- The Nordic countries, in particular Sweden, have instituted a parental leave which enables either one of the parents to take care of the young children at home; but it can be noted that very few fathers avail themselves of this opportunity.

- The status of a profession falls as the number of women entering it increases; salary levels thus become relatively less competitive. This trend is particularly clear in the teaching professions and in some medical professions.
- Measures of positive action are becoming more and more general. They cannot be successful unless they tackle discrimination on all fronts, together with the fixed ideas that are prevalent on the subject of the sexes. In fact, solutions to the financial problems that women's work causes are themselves going through an evolution in mentalities.

In a highly competitive job market, opportunities available to women are conditioned by the comparative cost of women's labour, as it is perceived by the employer. By virtue of the legislation in force in the majority of countries, the obligations linked to maternity protection and family responsibilities tend to increase the direct costs of women workers; generally, employers bridge this gap by lowering the wages of women or limiting recruitment to childless women. This form of discrimination can also go as far as requiring medical certificates to guarantee sterility.

A Global Programme

To avoid such tendencies, efforts should be channelled toward two fronts. First, the relationship between a real cost-benefit (including the criterion of effective productivity) with a view toward eliminating the false idea that women workers are more expensive.

Secondly, making sure that in legislation, in practice and especially in the mentality of men and women all round the reproductive function and care of persons are recognized as social functions whose costs should be footed by society as a whole.

Recognizing the universal nature of the problem and the various fronts where one would need to enter into combat, this programme should aim at changing the relationship of power between men and women. For this change to become permanent, it will be necessary to consolidate the ground gained as the process continues.

Remedies should be composed of measures touching upon, among other areas, legislation and its control, access to jobs, to training and to resources, the reconciling of professional activities with family responsibility, outreach measures to groups of underprivileged women, improvement of information and research, the participation of women in decision-making and the mobilization of public opinion.

18

The Dematerialisation of the World Economy

The first Industrial Revolution marked the transition from robber-and-plunder colonialism to the systematic development of the 'overseas' territories in the framework of an international division of labour between raw materials suppliers and manufacturers of finished goods. There was an 'historic integration' of the colonized areas in the development of their parent-states. What will the third Industrial Revolution do for the Third World? Will it now come to an 'historic separation'?

The end of the East-West conflict was reason enough to talk about a radical change in world politics. But at the same time an upheaval in the world economy is taking place that possibly will have even wider impacts. As a reference point for the following thoughts, three dimensions of this change are pointed out;

1. the upgrading of processing information rather than materials as object of economic activity (technological dimension);
2. the evolvement of global communications networks (sociocultural dimension);
3. the change of the nature of work (socio-economic dimension).

All three dimensions can be summarized under the buzzphrase 'tertialization of the world economy'.

In that respect, talk of the 'Third Industrial Revolution' is misleading. It is not about a third epoch of industrialization, but about the beginning of a de-industrialization, the transition from the industrial to the information society.

Historic Separation

In the 1960s and early 1970s, there was often talk of the Third World as the Third Sector of the world economy. Also then the Third World was not much more than an 'imaginary community'. But as such it had a certain significance in world politics. This implied not only its strategic role in the East-West conflict and its ideological function as the supporter of different 'third paths' between capitalism and socialism. It was also about the Third World's attested 'chaos power'. That linked the fear (in the North) and the hope (in the South) that the developing countries would be in a position to cut off the industrial nations from supplies of important raw materials, thus putting them under pressure. But it was soon seen that both sides had over estimated this possibility, even with regard to oil. Instead of supply bottlenecks arising, raw materials prices plummeted. For some commodities, the fall in prices exceeded those of the Great Depression of 1929/30.

This was due, *inter alia,* to the conjunction of lower demand from the industrial nations and expansion of production by the raw materials suppliers. Business activities dependent upon the supply of raw materials are tending to lose importance compared with the overall development of the global economy. The reason for this is to be seen in the transition from a material to an information economy.

This transition is taking place in line with the revolutionizing of data transmission and the expansion of financial transactions which are not directly related to changes in the production of materials. The speed of the changes is remarkable.

However, the dematerialization of business activities does not lead to decoupling in the Third World from the world economy. Declining market shares in world trade are not the expression of separation, but a loss of the affected countries positions in the world economy. Thus, the impact of dematerialization is 'only' that the negotiating positions of raw materials suppliers vis-a-vis the industrial nations will deteriorate further.

Differentiation of the Third World

But the radical change in the global economy is affecting some developing countries worse than others. Sub-Saharan Africa, and some countries in West and South Asia and Latin America are being pushed back further. The oil-producing countries with their high per capita export earnings will be able to hold their positions in the world economy for some time to come. The threshold countries of East and South-East Asia can expand theirs so long as they can continue to attract a growing share of global industrial production, and at the same time participate in the tertialization of the world economy in the shape of rapidly-growing financial transactions. Thereby it should be noted that the degree of tertialization in itself is not an adequate indicator for economic avant-gardism. Brazil exhibits a high degree of tertialization in combination with a low macroeconomic development dynamics. A good part of its tertialization is being achieved by speculative financial transactions with their inherently greater risks and uncertainties than in the industrial countries. Such dangers have been demonstrated by Mexico's peso crisis and its repercussions on the whole of Latin America.

In some Third World countries, a 'location annuity' has replaced the old raw materials one. Here it's about providing locations for off-shore transactions which offer international capital traders a maximum of freedom of movement combined with low taxation. Suitable for such operations are small countries which, despite low levy rates, achieve significant income in macroeconomic terms.

The radical changes in the world economy are spurring the differentiation of the Third World without, however, necessarily fostering a dissolution of the Third World as an 'imaginary community'. It is precisely the advanced countries of East and South-East Asia that are showing a certain interest in the formulation of joint positions of the 'South' in order to secure their own positional gains in the global economy. It's not by chance that the non-aligned countries and the Group of 77 have formed a joint coordination committee, and that the ASEAN countries are changing course on the international human rights policy.

Hitherto, the developing countries' strategy was to broaden the concept of human rights as a justification for demands on the industrial nations. But of late some developing countries, led by the ASEAN states, have questioned the universal validity of human rights even after their universality was confirmed by consensus at the Conference on Human Rights in Vienna in 1993. Playing a role in this policy is the governments' fear that due to the expansion of global communications networks, the behaviour patterns and preferences of their own people could in some way become similar to those of the West. As the rulers see it, that would be detrimental to the continuation of the development models practised so far.

Internet Creates New Cultural Dimension

Much information which Asian governments view as subversive is already globally available on the Internet. The old struggle over the world information order, which at first was primarily a clinch between East and West, is thus taking on a new dimension. For with the growing importance of computer literacy to a country's ability to assert itself on world markets, the Asian threshold countries have not only an interest in controlling the on-line communication but also to expand it and the know-how that it requires.

Even the critics of any interventions in the internet and other global communications networks must admit that modern communication technologies are politically blind and their use in itself does not represent progress. The setting up and expansion of global information highways will offer forum not only to people who want to use it for education and enlightenment, but also to all shades of fundamentalists. These highways will not necessarily bring the misery of many Third World regions closer to the industrial countries, but possibly rather strengthen the tendency to process all world events as entertainment.

Global Two-Thirds Society

The gravest aspect of the current upheaval in the world economy is its negative impact on jobs. The information economy needs for fewer workers than an economy based on materials. Instead, the demands on the skills of the workers are growing. Twenty per cent of the world workforce will in future be employed as (overworked) 'intelligence workers'. Eighty per cent will work part-time, if they are not underemployed or jobless. So the tertialization of the global economy delivers more underemployment rather than more leisure time. The workers who are rationalized out of their jobs in the industrial sector cannot be absorbed by the service sector because it, too, is not left untouched by rationalization measures. The civil service is also cutting back on staff. At all levels, there's a race to make the greatest possible savings on payrolls. At the same time, there's growing pressure to cut costs in providing for the victims of this development. That means thinning out the social security safety net.

The bottom line is that the two-thirds society, which developmental action groups hitherto assumed was limited to the Third World, is spreading worldwide. That, however, will not in the foreseeable future lead to an amendment of the North-South disparities. It's true that the change in the global economy is taking place faster and to a greater extent in the industrial nations. But rationalization is also happening in the developing countries in a bid to boost their competitiveness. So the upheaval in the world economy aggravates the problems which exist in a majority of the developing countries, while creating new ones in the industrial nations. The need for action on the North-South policy is growing, while the industrial nations. The need for action on the North-South Policy is growing, while the industrial nations' scope for concessions and compromises is shrinking. The new social question which is now crystallizing at global level is not being answered. The consequences are unforeseeable.

Another Loser?

It's more probable that a sharpening of the North-South confrontation is to be reckoned with. For the industrial nations will attempt to keep the social costs of the information economy at bay for as long as possible. The trade unions will thereby compete with the developing countries for jobs for their members. But this policy has its limits precisely because of the peaking of the problems in the industrial nations. Overstepping these limits means war, and passively accepting them chaos and social decay. Solutions could be sought in two directions: effective taxation of the information economies, and the creation of jobs in the non-profit sector. But it's possible there are no global solutions for global problems. That would mean for at least part of the Third World a renewal of the old debate on partial decoupling from the world economy.

19

Crisis and New Orientation of Development Policy

The poverty in the South, the dislocations in the East, and the orientation crisis in the North are not isolated phenomena. Rather, they represent an alarming amalgamation of dangers that are globally interlinked.

The low effectiveness of international economic and development policy is rooted in two outdated paradigms on which the present worldwide strategy of economic development is based, namely that:

1. The Western social and economic model optimizes the activation of productive forces—independent of the development stage of a country and its culture and therefore is best suited to satisfy basic needs.

2. It is possible to launch the development of a society from the outside within a few decades—without regard to its cultural and historical background—through external input of money, goods, technology, expertise, and personnel.

The twin paradigms of the timelessness and transferability combined with cultural ecological, and financial restrictions—have led international cooperation and development down the wrong path.

Only if we acknowledge the true dimensions of the global dangers, if we recognize the limitations and shortcomings of existing political instruments, and identify outdated theories and contradictory special interests, can we outline the cornerstones of a new policy of global cooperation.

Cornerstones of a New Development Policy

Starting with critical review of the shortcomings and paradigms of the prevailing development strategy, the following ten cornerstones of a new development policy are offered for discussion:

1. Broaden the Concept of Development

Whether a society is considered developed depends on the size of its per capita Gross National Product (GNP). Accordingly, the world is divided into a developed, semi-developed, and underdeveloped world. The yardstick for development, which has become the norm in the industrial countries, is one-dimensional: It only measures the monetary value of goods and services that are exchanged in the marketplace. This standard is too narrow economically because it compresses the multitude and complexity of cultural, societal, historical, social and human values into a single economic category.

At the most, there can be and should be agreement on what development and progress should not bring about: Inability to find enough work to meet the most basic needs; exploitation and oppression of people; loss of cultural wealth and institutions; destruction of natural resources. These, however, are the very values that are sacrificed by the prevailing development strategy. In the future, development policy must do all it can to stop the loss of skills and self-reliance, the plunder of natural resources, the erosion of cultural values, the violation of human dignity and human rights. Initiatives must prevail which are orientated on these values, and not just be the GNP.

2. Concentrate Development Strategy on the Internal Potential of Developing Countries

There must be an end to the manic fixation of development strategy on external inputs and external markets. A new development policy must, above all, improve internal conditions for a productive economy, promote domestic production factors on a broad basis, protect cultural and natural resources, and greatly increases the domestic supply of basic goods. Wherever external inputs and unavoidable, credits must be strictly tied to the productivity and the ability of a country to absorb transfers. External transfers should be concentrated on 'software' for health, education, social participation, administrative, and legal jurisdiction. Such an approach could also promote training and indigenous technologies, which are so important for economic development.

The set-up and expansion of the productive sectors must be decided, planned, and implemented by the developing countries themselves, and they must assume full responsibility. The external pressures, which force the developing countries into full integration with the world market, must be removed. This presupposes a structural reduction of interest rates.

3. Make Development Policy a Central Feature of Politics

Development policy must take the lead in mobilizing the various political forces and government departments to join the fight against the growing global dangers. It must ensure that the actions of all political departments are compatible with development policy is possible only if it becomes the central task of all political sectors, comparable to social and environmental policies, and the central goal of all policies. If development policy is to become a central task, development problems must become a priority in parliament and government. Society must understand that it is in the national interest to accept great global responsibilities.

4. Reform the World Economy

The industrial countries must abolish their protectionism in agriculture as well as the processed goods sector. Simultaneously, the developing countries need to be protected selectively and for a limited time against imports from the industrial countries. The undifferentiated structural adjustment policies imposed by the IMF must be revised. The trend toward regionalization of the world economy should not be opposed; rather, in the interest of both South and East, it must be regulated constructively to form a new, regionally based world trade structure.

A reform of the international finance system is urgently needed: Interest and exchange rates should not mirror the national interests of the big industrial states and the special interests of large banks and venture capital. Rather, they must reflect the global interest in monetary stability lower and stable interest rates; and sufficient development financing.

However, strengthening the international financial institutions is in the global interest only if the countries of the southern and eastern hemispheres are allowed to exert some influence. An international financial court must guarantee that violations of strict regulations to ensure international stability and solvency can be protested in a court of law.

5. Redesign the Industrial Society

As a global social and environmental policy, the new development policy must induce the industrial countries to give up their excessive consumption of air, water, soil, resources, and space. Increased utilization of energy-conservation measures and environmental friendly technologies is overdue. The economic and social policies of the industrial nations must promote balance rather than growth. This requires radical changes in traditional economic thinking, habits, structures and processes.

In view of limited world resources, unsatisfied existential needs in South and East, and continuous population growth in the South, the only premise for the future can be: Growth rates in the South must be higher than in the North, but they should no longer be in the North, but they should no longer be induced primarily by growth in the North. If economic policies continue to call for the North to provide the locomotive, the North will have to continue to acquire more resources than the South.

The North must relinquish the remaining growth frontiers to the South and East. The South must use this opportunity to activate its internal dynamic potential rather than integrate its economy with the North. However, ecological and social controls must be established at a much earlier stage than was the case in Europe.

6. Strengthen Development Cooperation

The share of official development assistance as a percentage of GNP, which dropped from 0.48 per cent in 1982 to 0.34 per cent in 1995 must be gradually raised against and reach at least 0.7 per cent in the year 2000—a goal which OECD established as early as to decades ago and which was reconfirmed at the Rio Earth Summit.

However, we must not succumb to the illusion that a doubling of ODA funds will even remotely meet the financial needs of South and East. State development policy must use its scarce public funds more effectively in the future. It must use restraint whenever partners in the developing countries can accomplish a task on their own and private initiatives and private enterprise are more competent to do the job. The government should be directly engaged only when it can be relatively more productive. Otherwise, it should limit itself to subsidizing private organisations.

7. New Orientation for Development Cooperation

The state and its implementation agencies must abandon all direct responsibility for any project which require unbureaucratic action, economic efficiency, and long term productivity. It must make a much greater effort to involve NGO's and private venture capital in development projects. At the same time, the state must insist and guarantee that private actions are compatible with social and ecological concerns.

In the future, the main thrust of government projects should be the promotion of the internal potential of a country. This comprises the political and administrative framework conditions of a humane, socially and ecologically sound development: Constitutional government, social institutions which facilitate broad participation of the population in politics, society, and economy; efficient savings, credit, fiscal and financial system; mechanisms for income, property, and land distribution which promote productivity, justice, and social peace. In addition of this 'software' of development, the following is needed: A regimen for the protection of resources and environment; measures to prevent the short term sellout of natural resources; elementary and general education and training, health care and social safety nets; capacities to develop science and technology.

8. Reduce the Debt Service and Activate Private Capital

Public funds must be used to a greater degree for the financial rehabilitation of highly indebted countries in South and East; external demands for interest and principal payments must be adapted to the economic capacity of the respective country and its ability to execute external capital transfers.

Within the frame work of international insolvency regulations, initiatives must be developed as a condition for the continuance of the present rules for write-offs-which ensure effective cooperation from the banks and alleviate the heavy burden of private credits, with their high interest rates.

State development policy and private business interests should supplement each other. Government promotion of private enterprise initiatives for exports, investment, and employment in the developing countries must take into account their compatibility with development. In reverse, private engagements which effectively promote development must be actively supported by the government. A separate line item must be established in the development budget for such activation of private capital.

9. Set Regional Priorities

State development cooperation has been scattering its scarce funds not only among too many sectors, but also among too many partners. In the future, public funds must be concentrated regionally. More emphasis must be placed on regional programmes, and development cooperation with threshold countries must be enhanced. A portion of public funds should be set aside to provide an incentive for be set aside to provide an incentive for threshold countries to assist the poorer nations in their own region as well as deal with poverty in their own country.

The new development policy could then also help lessen ethnic-national conflicts and promote peace by sponsoring regional cooperation in joint development projects. For this purpose, regional development funds must be set up for cooperation in the transportation, energy, trade, and finance sectors and last, but not least for regional security systems and disarmament. Such regional funds could also provide the means to project refugees and improve their prospects for an eventual return to their homelands.

20

Development: The Third Way

While great claims are being made for the increasingly more efficient and effective technologies perfected to serve development of the people in this scientific age, huge problems are threatening the globe. The problems are mass poverty and hunger, underdevelopment, waste, unemployment, resource scarcity, environmental destruction and armed conflict.

In finding answers to the prevailing problems we must be clear about the meaning and purpose of development. The first glaring mistake made is that development is interpreted as development of the economy and not as the total development of society. When economic development is made the supreme goal, most of the other vital aspects get ignored, namely, development of the political system, community, social cohesion, the ecology, culture and values, Development and stability go hand in hand while poverty and chaos constitute the antithetical twin.

Appropriate Development

The key elements in the conception of appropriate, development consist of: first, aiming at sufficiently comfortable material living standards and not affluent standards of the rich as in prosperous nations. Second, development must not be confused with GNP growth. Mere increase of economic activity must not be pursued exclusively at the cost of articles that are urgently needed by the poor majority to maintain them at a reasonable level of material living. Third, in the villages, we must produce articles as are needed by the villagers. Fourth grassroots and participatory development is essential so that the local people identify and solve their local problems. Fifth, instead of capital and energy intensive high technology, use labour-intensive technology, Instead of heavy industrialization, promote medium scale industries and technologies. And, sixth, instead of preoccupation with a high GNP growth rate, focus on the development of communities and of rural bodies and take care to conserve the local ecosystems. The main purpose should be to meet the primary needs of ordinary people and promotion of their productive resources such as land.

In developing countries like India where billions of poor people remain condemned by conventional economic development strategies and theories, it is vital to introduce appropriate development measures to remove deprivation and ensure the necessity of modest living standards.

The world has witnessed the operation of the two systems namely, the capitalist and the socialist one that have obtained in different countries. Although both the systems have underlined the welfare of all as the basic goal, both have left a legacy of waste, hunger and gross human inequality. Some 1000 million people do not get enough to eat including some 20 million in the USA.

Third World Way of Development

The iniquitous situation in the present day world has sparked off fierce controversies among the conventional economists and the new radical economists who champion a third way, as the alternative way to serve the primary goal of all humanity to have sufficient means to lead a comfortable peaceful life.

In order to achieve prosperity, conventional economists have emphasized the production of bigger cake on the assumption that everyone will get a slice of it. They also argue that a 'tide will lift all the boats'. Both these assumptions have proved false in that the poor have neither the slice of cake nor has their boat been lifted. Third way system lays stress on highly localized, less cash-reliant and simply structured set-up. It should not be dependent on transport of goods, but concentrate or more local production to meet local needs with a role for barter and free exchange. He urges a radical re-think of conventional economics.

Is this Stepping Backwards?

The most common criticism levelled against the Third Way is that it will arrest the progress made hitherto and that it might mean a return to a 'primitive' way of life. There should be no fear on this score because the Third Way aims at the reduction in the use of resources and therefore, of excessive production and consumption. It does not in any sense mean stepping backwards to a lower level of the quality of life. Nor is the alternative way intended to destroy capitalism or socialism. The conception of the alternate way is to promote economic growth compatible with capitalism and socialism. The ground idea is to promote selflessness, mutual concern and social responsibility. This will replace selfish, competitive and avaricious attitudes as have developed in the conventional economic order of today.

NGO's Resolution at the Rio Conference

That there is increasing awareness of the threat posed by the growing power of multinational corporations was articulated by the international NGO forum in its Declaration resolved on 12 June 1992 at the UN Conference of Environment and development in Rio de Janeiro. The Declaration states that "the Bretton Woods institutions have served the major instruments by which the destruction policies have been imposed on the world" and calls upon "the world's people to protect their economic, social, cultural and environmental interests against the growing power of transnational capital". The declaration further avers "we recognize the central place of spiritual values and spiritual development... and values of simplicity, love, peace, and reverence for life.

After the failure of the socialist system over four decades to achieve prosperity for all, the Indian Government switched over to the global market economy and is steaming ahead with added liberalization measures to attract foreign investment and the multinational corporations (MNCs). Some adverse effects of this are already visible: for example, majority financial equity granted to MNCs and the emergence of foreign subsidiaries with cent per cent financial equity; the introduction of Pizza and Kentucky Fried Chicken which has been detested by the people in Karnataka. The farmers have also revolted because their rights to produce and sell seeds have been wrested by foreign MNCs who have acquired patent rights over certain Indian crop seeds. In this scenario, the Third Way has much to commend itself to the Government. The Third Way has the air of the Gandhian model of economy and production which emphasizes production by people for their own needs and preference for small and medium sized industry. The same paradigm was championed by the renowned economist Schumacher when he said 'Small is beautiful'. India should take good care against the present-day headlong drive for the entry of foreign capital and foreign heavy industries.

21

Violence in Schools: A World Wide Affair

In all countries, schools are magnets for strife in society. Dealing with these tensions calls for extreme caution, for fear of making matters worse. Violence in schools is a world wide problem: it exists in rich and poor countries alike. It's chiefly a male phenomenon, hitting a peak when boys turn 16 years old in some countries and 13 in others. Experts agree at least on one point: this violence cannot be pinned to a single cause. Instead, they point to complex patterns linked to family situations. Socio-economic conditions and teaching methods.

Tackling Segregation

But these are just indicators and do not justify any deterministic explanations. When researchers say that 10 to 20 per cent of risk factors are linked to single parent families, this suggests that 80 to 90 per cent of such families are not the source of any violence. A child from a slum area with a teenage mother or a father in jail will not automatically be violent! Likewise, experts say there is a 'hard core' of violent children—about five per cent of the total. One can found that this figure can vary between one and 11 per cent. The school itself can be an aggravating factor, through high staff turnover or 'ghetto classes' to which poorly-performing students are relegated. These 'hard core' groups, then, cannot be deemed 'inalterable'. On the contrary, something can be done about them.

Should they simply be expelled, as some advocate? Such a measure would only make their segregation and sense of exclusion worse. And they are, after all, at the root of the whole problem. The solution lies partly in developing customized projects, but most importantly, in strengthening economic social participation.

To put an end to school violence, we need a well-established state with the means to compensate for inequalities, a state that tries to re-establish diversity in neighbourhoods and schools, one that does not give up on the notion of justice for children, as some are demanding.

Passing the Torch:

We should also try to lift schools out of their fortresses, so they do not become the symbol of a society that excludes people. Projects in the Netherlands, Brazil and the United States have shown that schools can be vibrant places that provide social, medical and cultural services to a neighbourhood.

In the Brazilian state of Minas Gerais, for example, there is a vocational school where elderly craftsmen teach their skills to teenagers. Such contact between generations can offer a very valuable social education. "It takes a village to educate a child", goes an effort an African proverb. Let's make an effort to seek out these opportunities, even in the most heartless cities.

22

Do Men Matter?

New Horizons in Gender and Development

Why do men not feature more in gender and development policy? The shift in emphasis from Women in Development (WID) to Gender and Development (GAD), from enumerating and redressing women's disadvantages to analysing the social relationships between men and women, has not led to a recognition within policy of the need to understand the position of women and men. Is there a need for an explicit focus on men in GAD?

With a few notable exceptions, men are rarely explicitly mentioned in gender policy documents. Where men do appear, they are generally seen as obstacles to women's development; men must surrender their positions of dominance for women to become empowered. The superiority of women as hard working, reliable trustworthy, socially responsible, caring and co-operative is often asserted, whilst men on the other hand are frequently portrayed as lazy, violent promiscuous and irresponsible drunkards.

Why, then, focus on men? Emerging critiques of policy argue for special attention to be paid to men and masculinities in development as follows:

Gender is Relational

It concerns the relationships between men and women which are subject to negotiation in private and public spheres. To focus on women only is inadequate; a better understanding of men's perceptions and positions and the scope for changing these, is essential. Exploring masculinities' includes focusing on socially constructed ways of being a man 'rather than simply on their physical and sexual attributes, Biological essentialism is rejected in favour of an analysis of the social context within which gendered roles and relations are formed.

Equality and Social Justice

Gender concerns should not simply be viewed as instrumental in securing a more effective delivery of development. Instead, this critique recognises that men as well as women may be disadvantages by social and economic structures and that they both have the right to live free from poverty and repression. Empowerment processes should also enable women and men to be liberated from the confines of gender stereotyped roles.

Gendered Vulnerabilities

Evident from several studies suggests that while women in general may face greater social and economic disadvantages, men are not always the winners and that generalising about their situation risks overlooking gender-specific inequities and vulnerabilities, such as the damaging health effects of certain 'masculine' labour roles or social practices.

Crisis of Masculinity

It is suggested that changes in the economy, social structures, and household composition are resulting in crisis of masculinity in many parts of the world. The 'demasculinising' effects of poverty and of economic and social change may be eroding men's traditional roles as providers and limiting the availability of alternative, meaningful roles for men in families and communities. Men may consequently seek affirmation of their masculinity in other ways, through irresponsible sexual behaviour or domestic violence for example.

Strategic Gendered Partnerships

There is a strong argument that if gender equitable changes is to be achieved in households, communities and organisations, then surely men are needed as allies and partners? This links to concerns about the need to mainstream gender issues in development policy to ensure that they are not sidelined or under-funded as 'women's issues'.

Men and masculinities is a relatively new era in gender and development. Ideas concerning policy implications are in their infancy. How can research, policy, and training contribute to the debate and complete the shift from WID to GAD so that the situation of women and men is better understood? Suggestions include:

- investigating the changing roles, needs and identities of men over life courses;
- researching men's roles in families, the reproduction of gender inequities through work, and men's specific health vulnerabilities;
- tracking and monitoring changes in gender relationships over time, in different cultural contexts, in association with programmes and policies;
- developing positive role models for men and boys influencing mass media images, establishing activities in schools, NGOs, religious and youth groups;
- ensuring the legal frameworks supports gender equity, through regulating working hours, parental leave provision, improved maintenance and inheritance law for example;
- improving gender training within development organisations to focus on gender and not women alone: for example by increasing the number of male gender trainers and improving gender analysis frameworks.

23

People as Hostages

The Humanitarian Consequences of Sanctions

Following the end of the Cold War, the UN was able to rediscover and impose the sanctions provided for by Article 41 of the UN Charter to maintain or restore international peace and security. Whereas during the preceding decades the UN Security Council had applied such non-military coercive measures only twice, against Rhodesia and South Africa, sanctions have been imposed more than ten times since 1989. The targets: Iraq, Yugoslavia, Somalia, Liberia, Libya, Haiti, Angola, Rwanda, Sudan, Afghanistan, and Sierra Leone. There is now enough experience of the useful and harmful impacts of sanctions to be able to assess the feasibility of this instrument and suggest reforms. That applies also to the bilateral sanctions imposed by the USA.

The Impact of Sanctions

The application of sanctions is at first accompanied with hopes, which are followed mostly by disappointment and sometimes by abhorrence. The hopes are based on the belief that sanctions still can prevent an armed conflict by making a targeted country drop its belligerent attitude due to its leaders listening to reason or responding to the pressure of their people. Disappointment arises from the unreliable calculation of political success, from considerations of legitimacy, and from the problems of affected third countries. Abhorrence is triggered by the ethical dilemma that the suffering caused by sanctions has a greater impact on the ordinary people than upon the political elite, making them hostages to the confrontation.

To be sure, the UN organs, the Security Council is a political rather than a judicial or humanitarian organ of the international community. It does not have to observe the principle of equal treatment and can react differently to developments in Haiti than to those in Nigeria or Burma, to say nothing about Chechnya. But like all UN organs, the Security Council is bound to overarching principles. These include in particular respect for human rights, which it must bear in mind in considering the consequences of its actions.

From a developmental viewpoint, it is worrying to note that sanctions are targeted almost solely on countries of the South. That is just as questionable as the damage suffered by the neighbours and trade partners of countries under sanctions. That applies, for instance, to the Danube littoral states in the case of Yugoslavia, and to Jorden in the case of the sanctions against Iraq.

Furthermore, one of the other drawbacks in wielding the sanctions instrument is the longstanding practice of imposing them on an open-ended basis. That means a country can rid itself of sanctions only with great effort because the veto of a single permanent member of the Security Council can prevent them from being lifted. If sanctions were in future imposed for fixed periods, it would require a fresh Security Council decision to reapply them. Given this process, the sanctions against Libya, for example, would have ended much earlier.

Finally, it is hard to bear that some major powers instrumentalise the Security Council for their own purposes, such as the USA in its quarrel with Libya. Leading Western new media covering the Lockerbie trial in The Netherlands were means-while drip-feeding their public with selective information from secret service circles to prepare them for the news that Libyan involvement in the bomb blast which brought down the Pan Am airliner over Scotland was unlikely to be proven.

Discussion in the UN

The recommendations of UN Secretary-general for many years for more care in applying the sanctions instrument correspond to a widely-held view in the UN. For instance, Boutros Boutros-Ghali called in his annex to the UN's Agenda for Peace of January 1995 for a 'mechanism' to assess and examine the consequences of sanctions. And in Kofi Annan's Millennium Report of April 2000, he called on the UN heads of state and government leaders to agree on measures to make economic sanctions adopted by the Security Council impact less harshly on innocent populations, and more effective in bringing pressure to bear on target regimes. The international Red Cross and other humanitarian aid organisations have for years made similar statements.

First and foremost, it is about avoiding so-called humanitarian consequences. In 1997 the UN did, in fact, cancel implementation of an agreed flight ban against Sudan due to an expert report which forecast such impacts. That is distinct progress. It also shows that as a rule it is not a matter of unforeseen or unintended impacts in the sense of 'collateral damage', but about the acceptance of foreseeable and deliberate consequences. For the contrast to the rules of warfare, which primarily should not be waged against the civil population, the logic of sanction impacts is based on their intended effect on the people of the target country. Their morale is to be broken, making them exert internal pressure on their rulers.

The Case of Iraq

Humanitarian consequences arise above all when comprehensive economic sanctions are imposed which, as in the cases of Iraq and Yugoslavia, ban international trade, transport and financial transactions. That means infant and child mortality, hunger, sickness and human misery: impacts that are visibly and measurably a danger to life.

Certainly, causalty in individual cases is an area of dispute. Iraq is a clear example of that. The sanctions against it are affecting a population that in a short time have lived through two terrible and bloody wars involving heavy losses, and whose ruler obviously does not give top priority to the immediate basic needs of his people. So there is more than one reason for the misery. But mutual apportioning of blame can exculpate no-one. Whoever creates conditions that cause innocent children to die cannot with a clear conscience claim that others have done that too. The US and Iraqi governments, however, are so deeply hostile to each other that even taking an objective view of the situation in the interest of the people affected is judged as taking sides.

At any rate, sanctions contribute a great deal to worsen a people's plight. Unfortunately the international debate on sanctions tends so settle for demanding a guarantee of access for humanitarian aid. The Security Council resolutions contain corresponding exemption provisions. Demarcations in the sector of 'dual use' goods have also become somewhat more sensible since the days when Winston Churchill argued that war material could be made even from food. Foodstuffs and medical supplies are expected from the embargo. But that does not solve the humanitarian problem. As we unfortunately note constantly, the aid available around the world is not enough to provide sufficient help in all emergency and disaster situations. That means the people of an internationally outlawed country can expect even less assistance.

An especially annoying circumstance in the case of Iraq was that its own rich resources were not allowed to be used for emergency aid. The 'oil-for-food' programme approved by the UN in 1996 was supposed to remedy that to a limited extent. But few people know that only part of the proceeds from Iraq's oil sales is available for humanitarian purposes because sums to compensate victims of Iraq's aggression against Kuwait and pay off UN costs and deducted first. Still, the aid is useful and has resulted in a certain improvement in supply. Whoever reports that must expect censure from those critics of the UN for whom the fact that aid is reaching the people affected does not fit their negative enemy image.

The debate on whether the sanctions against Iraq have led to a three-fold or five-fold increase in child mortality can be left to the experts. Rightly, UNICEF, the WHO and others have highlighted these figures because they in particular grab public attention. But one should realise that these statistics are only an indication of the dreadful worsening of the overall health situation of the people of Iraq over the last decade. Before the Gulf War, Iraq was relatively prosperous, its public health service was well staffed and well equipped and able to offer the people comprehensive free healthcare at a good level, it is now totally ruined. Malnutrition and poor drinking water quality have led to an increase in many illnesses on a sometimes-epidemic scale. Hospitals are unable to function due to a lack of equipment and medicines.

The decline of the public health service is in turn also only an indication of the general shortcomings in Iraq that is expressed equally in a run-down school system, widespread unemployment and other social dislocation such as the gradual disappearance of small to medium-sized businesses and an increase in crime.

Reform Proposals are on the Table

Three years ago, a group of American academics presented a list of indicators aimed at helping to establish the starting point and impact of sanctions in the social sector. Among other things, it was meant to point out the vulnerabilities of endangered sections of populations and enable recommendations for the design of sanction regimes. The report offered some telling and cogent indicators for the sectors of public health, the economy, migration movements, politics and humanitarian aid. Most of these indicators were registered by UN specialist organisations. The intention now is to incorporate such information as standards in the consultation and decision processes of the Security Council.

For here it is a question of fundamental human rights which the international community must respect. The people threatened or affected by sanctions have compelling rights (jus cogens). First of all, these are the right to life, good health, food, water, housing and clothing. Starving a people must never be permitted. The limits of sanctions are clearly overstepped when a considerable section of the population drops below the subsistence level. With regard to Iraq, there has been growing criticism in recent years that the Security Council has not met fully its responsibility for the consequences of its actions. The UN's economic sanctions were at any rate from the time that they led to life-threatening impacts for the Iraqi civil population, and in particular to an empirically verifiable reduction of life expectancy due to lack of and under-supply of the people, as well as an increase in child mortality, a violation of the right to life and thus are to be judged as unlawful.

It is morally and legally untenable to treat the people of so-called 'rogue states' inhumanly or to make humanitarian aid subject to political changes, as recently in Yugoslavia. Whoever does that is himself a rogue. Sanctions must not be used, as to date, as what Boutros-Ghali called a 'blunt instrument'. They should above all hit decision-takers and political elites. 'Smart sanctions' are called for, and are being discussed keenly at international conferences. 'Scalpel rather than a cudgel' is the motto.

24

Crisis Prevention

Can Better Development Planning Lessen the Toll of Civil Emergencies and Natural Disasters

Even a cursory scan of the world's headlines is depressing: armed conflicts are grinding on the Somalia, Afghanistan and in a growing number of other countries. And the effects of natural disasters are becoming more catastrophic each year. International relief aid, in response to such emergencies, has increased substantially. But how large can these sums of money realistically be expected to grow? With no end in sight to the need for relief, the good will of international donors is quickly giving way to disillusionment.

This leads us to a second question, which is, where does development fit in this grim scenario? For the development community to remain aloof from the issue of disasters and emergencies is not only politically short-sighted, it also ignores totally the causes and the effects of such phenomena.

Natural hazards such as hurricanes and earthquakes may be impossible to prevent. But they only become natural disasters if people are vulnerable. Why is it, for example, that an earthquake in Khilari, Maharashtra that registered 6.9 on the Richter scale killed up to 35,000 people, when an earthquake of almost the exact same magnitude in Los Angeles in 1994 claimed only 57 lives? By reducing poverty we can help increase the coping capacity of vulnerable populations. Therefore helping people lower such vulnerability is as much a development issue as the environment, or women's participation in development. Moreover, the repercussions of natural disasters go far beyond the immediate casualty list that so transfixes the media. Secondary and longer-term effects can be equally if not more devastating. And they must be taken into account by development practitioners.

It has been estimated, for example, that the damage to Mexico City's infrastructure form a massive 1985 earthquake amounted to US$ 3.6 billion. Yet over the subsequent five years, the negative ripple effect on that country's balance of payments resulted in a loss of $8.6 billion. Furthermore, reconstruction requirements forced Mexican authorities to revise their economic policies to meet an increased demand for public funding, credits and imports. The priorities for public expenditure were redirected to reconstruction projects, leaving many of the pre-disaster problems of the city and its people unattended.

In Bangladesh, floods in the recent past 2,000 people. But on closer examination we find that the toll was much more extensive than that: in each of these years that country's economic growth rate was halved by the delayed planting of rice and the destruction of seedbeds in the floods, further undermining the country's food security. All of these are consideration that go beyond relief, but they must be taken into account by development professionals.

Other emergencies may be more complex, but must be subjected to the same analysis. As the situations in Angola, Burundi, Somalia and the former Yugoslavia demonstrate, we know little about the dynamics of emergencies that arise from civil conflict. We do know, however that their cause usually lies in a lethal mix of poverty, poor governance and ethnic or religious rivalries exacerbated by profound social inequities. We are also learning that their resolution frequently requires the application of peacekeeping and political measures, combined with relief and development.

Among the most virulent effects of such complex emergencies is the massive displacement of people; women and children are the principal victims, constituting 70 per cent of the world's refugees.

These complex emergencies around the world could easily get worse before they get better. This being said, carefully designed development efforts-carried out as building blocks to national reconciliation in the fragile post-conflict stage will need to increase commensurately. The appropriateness and the sustainability of these development efforts will be one of the most important factors in determining whether peace itself becomes sustainable. For example, the absence of carefully tailored reintegration strategies for demobilized soldiers and their host communities would be an almost open invitation to resumed violence.

Yet we must also be conscious of the impact of aid and try harder to prevent the need for relief in the first place. An increasing body of evidence suggests, for example that emergency aid can sometimes be counter-productive in the longer term, increasing the vulnerability of populations and impeding recovery. Ironically, we find ourselves in situation today where it is far easier to obtain funds for maintaining refugees in their places of asylum than for helping them reintegrate into their own societies. In such cases, we may very well be helping to perpetuate the problem that we sought to relieve, as the presence of large numbers of refugees is sometimes itself a cause of conflict.

So how are we to proceed? And what exactly is the nature of the relief to development continuum that remains logical in the abstract but elusive in reality? The concept of a continuum does not imply a linear and absolutely progressive set of responses. On the contrary, it means that we are dealing with a set of processes rather than rigidly defined steps. It also means that development must be very much part of the disaster management process, and that the aim of the continuum must be to move from relief to rehabilitation and resumed development at the earliest opportunity. However, this resumed development must include conscious measures to reduce the vulnerability that caused the disaster or the emergency in the first place.

In other words, we must give greater thought to prevention before we reach for the 'cure'—for humanitarian, political and financial reasons. (The Japanese insurance industry spends $ 200 million a year on disaster education alone). And as development practitioners, we must reconcile ourselves to the vastly more complicated environment in which we have to operate.

This means, for example that we will have to begin examining whether the economic policy 'medicine' often prescribed will reduce conflict or enhance it. We will have to ask ourselves if the reconstruction period following a civil conflict or natural disaster is the right time to advocate cuts in social spending, as has happened in certain countries in Africa and Latin America. Similarly, is it really in children's best interests to build a school in a seismic zone without first ensuring its structural stability? And does it really make sense to urge drought-prone countries to increase their reliance on cash crops as has been done in some instances.

A story that never made headlines anywhere involves hundreds of the poorest people in Bangladesh, whose homes remained intact during the floods of 1988, when many others were simply washed away. These people were fortunate enough to have obtained credit through the Grameen Bank for construction materials as well as instruction in the building of flood-resistant homes. The Grameen revolving fund had received start-up capital from International Financial Agencies. Since that time the effort has been expanded, and more than 10,500 flood-resistant homes have been built in the last two years.

This is just one example of the kind of action we need more of—in fairly predictable and recurring circumstances such as the floods in Bangladesh, as well as in the more complex, man-made emergencies to which we must respond.

BIBLIOGRAPHY

Ackoff, R.L., *Redesigning the Future: A Systems Approach to Societal Problems* (John Wiley, 1974).

Adelman, I., *et. al. Economic Growth and Social Equality in Developing Countries* (California, Standford University, 1967).

Aggarwal, Y.P., *Education and Human Resource Development* (New Delhi, Commonwealth, 1988).

Amirk Singh., 'New Policy on Education: Two Years Later', *Economic and Political Weekly*, Special Number, Vol. XXIII, Nos. 45, 46 and 47, pp. 2479-92.

Anand, Mulk Raj, 'A Nation of Illiterates' *The Tribune*. Feb. 12, 1991.

Anderson, C.A., 'A Skeptical Note on Education and Mobility', A.H. Halsey, and Others (ed)—*Education Economy and Society*, (New York, The Free Press, 1969), pp. 164-182.

Anderson, C.A., 'Access to Higher Education and Economic Development' in *Halsey, A.H. (Ed)-op. cit.* work. pp. 252-268.

Anderson, C.A., and Bowman, M.J., *Education and Economic Development* (Chicago, 1965).

Anon, 'The Pressure of Economic Change' in A.H. Halsey, (Ed), *op. cit.* pp. 22-30.

Anon, 'All-out Bid to Tap Human Resources', *The Economic Times* (Supplement), Dec. 20, 1984, pp. 1-3.

Asharaya, P., 'Education: Politics and Social Structure', *Economic and Political Weekly*, Vol. XX, No. 42, Oct. 19, 1985, pp. 1785-89.

Bantock, G.A., *Education and Values,* (London, Faber and Faber, 1966).

Bauer, R.A. (Ed), *Social Indicators* (Cambridge and London, MIT Press, 1966).

Becker, Garry S., *Human Capital* (Princeton, Princeton University Press, 1964).

Becker, Garry S., *Human Capital: A Theoretical and Empirical Analysis with Special Reference to Education,* (New York, NBER, 1974).

Ben-Porath, Yoram. 'The Production of Human Capital and the Life Cycle of Earnings', *The Journal of Political Economy,* August, 1967, pp. 352-65.

Benson, Charles S. *Perspectives on the Economics of Education* (Boston, Houghton Mifflin Company, 1963).

Bhalla, G.S. and Bhalla, H.S. 'Human Resource Development for Rural Poor', Paper presented at the *U.G.C. National Seminar,* held at G.K.I.A.S. in Rural Development, Punjabi University; Campus, Damdama Sahib).

Bhatia, S.K., 'Challenges in Human Resource Management' *Indian Management,* Vol. 25, No. 8, August 1986, pp. 5-12.

Blaug, Mark (Ed), *Economics of Education-I* (New York, Penguin, 1968).

Blaug, Mark (Ed), *Economics of Education-II* (New York, Penguin, 1969).

Blaug, Mark, *An Introduction to the Economics of Education* (New York, Penguin, 1970).

Blaug, Mark, 'The Empirical Status of Human Capital Theory: Slightly Jaundiced Survey', *Journal of Economic Literature,* Vol. 14, No. 3, September 1976, pp. 827-55.

Boulding, K., *The Meaning of the Twentieth Century* (London, Allen and Unwin, 1965).

Bowman, M.J., 'Education and Economic Growth *in King, I. (Ed), Education and Income* (Staff Working Paper No. 402, Washington, World Bank, 1980) pp. 1-71.

Bowman, M.J., 'The Human Investment Revolution in Economic Thought', *Sociology of Education* 39/2 (Spring), pp. 111-37.

Brown, Murraya (Ed), *The Theory and Empirical Analysis of Production* (New York, NBER, 1967).

Brownstein, L., *Education and Development in Rural Kenya* (New York, Praeger, 1972).

Burgess, T. et al., *Manpower and Educational Development in India* (London, Oliver and Boynd).

Byars, L.L. and Rue, L.W., *Human Resource Management* (Illinois, Irwin Homewood).

Chattopadhyay, G., 'Education: The Authority to Learn or the Authority of the Bowl of Hemlock' in *Decision* (IIM, Calcutta), Vol. 16, No. 1, Jan-March, 1989, pp. 22-33.

Cheema, C.S. 'The Challenges of Human Resource Development in Rural Punjab'—Paper presented at *U.G.C. National Seminar* held at G.K.I.A.S. in Rural Development, Punjabi University Campus, Damdama Sahib).

Clark, Harold F., 'The Return on Educational Investment' in C.S. Benson, (Ed), *op. cit.*, 1963, pp. 24-32.

Coombs, P.H. and Manzoor Ahmed, *Attacking Rural Poverty: Non-Formal Education Can Help* (John Hopkins University Press, 1974).

Coombs, P.H., *The World Crisis in Education: The View from Eighties* (Oxford, OUP, 1985).

Correa, Hector, *The Economics of Human Resources* (Amsterdam, North-Holland, 1963).

Curle, Adam, 'Some Aspects of Educational Planning in Underdeveloped Areas, *Harvard Educational Review,* Vol. 32, No. 3, 1962.

D'Souza, A.A. and De Souza., A. *Population Growth and Human Development* (Delhi, ISI, 1974).

Datta, S., 'Human Resource Development', *Man and Development*, Vol. 8, No. 1, March 1986, pp. 9-17.

Davis, R.G., *Planning Human Resource Development*, (Chicago, 1966).

Davis, Russel G. *Planning Human Resource Development: Education Models and Schemata* (Chicago, CSED, Harvard University, 1966).

Denison, Edward F., 'Education and Growth' in Benson, C.S. (Ed), *op. cit.*, pp. 33-42.

Desai A.R. *Social Background of Indian Nationalism* (Bombay, Popular, 1966).

Deshmukh, C.D. 'Management and Administration: New Trends', *Training Abstracts 17*, New Delhi Training Division, 1972.

Dey, B., 'On Costing Education' in Pandit's *Measurement of Cost Productivity and Efficiency of Education* (New Delhi, NCERT, 1969), pp. 14-26.

Dey, B. 'Training in the Civil Services: Plea for A Holistic Construal', *Indian Journal of Public Administration* Vol. XXIV, No. 4, Oct.-Dec. 1982.

Drucker, Peter F. 'The Educational Revolution' in Halsey and Others (Ed) *op. cit.*, pp. 15-21.

Drucker, Peter, F., *Managing in Turbulent Times* (William Heinemann, 1980).

Dwivedi, R.S., *Management of Human Resources: A Behavioural Approach to Personnel* (New Delhi, Oxford and IBH, 1982).

Farooq, Khan A., 'Development of Human Resources', *The Economic Times*, September 22, 1984.

Gandhi, Rajiv, 'New National Policy on Education', *Inaugural Address* at the Conference of Education Ministers at New Delhi, August 29, 1985.

Gill, K.S., 'Agricultural Development in Punjab' in Johar and Khanna's (Ed), *Studies in Punjab Economy* (Amritsar, GNDU, 1983).

Gore, M.S., 'Literacy: Equaliser of Opportunity', *Democratic World,* March 31, 1991, Vol. XX. No. 13.

Gostkowski, Z., *Towards A System of Human Resources Indicators for Less-Developed Countries* (The Polish Academy of Sciences).

Government of India, *Challenges of Education: A Policy Perspective* (Government of India, Ministry of Education, 1985).

Government of India, *National Policy on Education* (New Delhi, Govt. of India, 1986).

Government of India, *National Policy on Education: Programme of Action* (New Delhi, Govt. of India, 1986).

Groves, Harold M., 'Education and Economic Growth' in C.S. Benson, (Ed), *op. cit.*, pp. 7-11.

Halsey, A.H. and Others (Ed), *Education, Economy and Society* (New York, The Free Press, 1969).

Harbison, F., 'The Prime Movers of Innovations' in Halsey, A.H. and Others (Ed) *op. cit.*

Harbison, F. *Human Resources as the Wealth of Nations* (London, OUP, 1973).

Harbison, F. and Myers, C. A. *Education, Manpower and Economic Growth* (New York, 1974).

Havighurst, R.J., 'Education and Social Mobility' in Four Societies' in A.H. Halsey, and Others (Ed), *op. cit.*, pp. 105-120.

Heyneman, S.P., *Improving the Quality of Education in Developing Countries* (Washington, World Bank, 1983).

Heyneman, S.P. and White, D.S., *The Quality of Education and Economic Development* (Washington, World Bank, 1986).

Hicks, Norman, *Economic Growth and Human Resources*, World Bank, Staff Paper No. 408, (Washington, World Bank, 1980).

Hilton School of. *Human Resource Development* (Vellore, ISSR, 1989).

Huq, M.S., *Education, Manpower and Development in South and South-East Asia* (Delhi, Sterling, 1975).

Hussain, Majid, *Agricultural Geography* (New Delhi, Inter-India, 1986).

Jagannathan, N., 'Gender Equality in Education', *University News*, Vol. XXIX, No. 5, Feb. 4, 1991, pp. 1-5.

Jamison, D.T. and Laurence, J.L., *Farmer Education and Farm Efficiency* (Baltimore, John Hopkins, 1982).

Jhingan, M.L., *The Economics of Development and Planning* (New Delhi, Vikas, 1975).

Jhonson, D. Gale., 'Economics and the Educational System, in C.S. Benson, (Ed), *op. cit.*, pp. 374-80.

Joshi, P.C., 'Role of Culture in Social Transformation and National Integration, *Economic and Political Weekly*, Vol. XXI, No. 28.

Kamat, A.R., *Progress of Education in Rural Maharashtra* (Pune, Gokhale Institute of Politics and Economics, 1968).

Khanna, G., Parkash, S. and Bansal, R.K., *Unit Cost of College Education in Punjab* (Patiala, Punjabi University, 1985) mimeo.

Khullar, K.K., 'Four Decades of Education', *Yojana*, Vol. 33, No. 8, Nov. 1-15, 1989, pp. 12-4.

King, T. (Ed)., *Education and Income*, World Bank Staff Working, Paper No. 402, Washington, World Bank, 1980.

Kirpal, P. 'How To Plan Education of The Future', *Yojana,* Vol. 33, No. 14 and 15, August, 1989.

Kothari, Commission, *Report of the Education Commission: 1964-66* (Delhi, Government of India, 1970).

Kothari, V.N. and Panchamukhi, P.R., 'Economics of Education: A Trend Report' in *ICSSR's A Survey of Research in Economics* (New Delhi, 1980), pp. 169-238.

Krishnamurthy, H.V. 'Human Resource Development Strategy For 21st Century; *P.U. Management Review*, Vol. 9, Nos. 1 and 2, Jan.-Feb. 1986, pp. 79-89.

Kulkarni, V.G. 'Alternatives in Education' *Man and Development* (Vol. VIIII), March 1985, pp. 25-58.

Lipton, *Why Poor Stay Poor: A Study of Urban Bias in World Development* (London, Templesmith, 1977).

MacNamara, R.S. *The Assault on World Poverty* (Washington, World Bank, 1975).

Mahajan, V.S. 'Whither National Policy: Education', *The Tribune*, Feb. 24, 1991, p. 8.

Majumdar, Tapas. *Investment in Education and Social Choice*, (New York, Cambridge University Press, 1983).

Marshall, Alfred. 'Education and Invention' in Benson, C.S. (Ed), *op. cit.*, pp. 82-83.

Mathur, B.L. (Ed)., *Human Resource Development: Strategic Approaches and Experiences*, (Jaipur, Arihant, 1989).

Mathur, R.N., *Population Analysis and Studies* (Allahabad, Chugh).

Megginson, L.C., *Personnel and Human Resource Administration*, 1974.

Mehta, M.M., *Human Resource Development Planning*, (Delhi, Macmillan, 1976).

Mingat, Alan and Tan, Jee-Pang. *Analytical Tools for Sector Work in Education* (Baltimore/London, John Hopkins University Press, 1988).

Mishra, L. 'Literacy: Now or Never' in *Yojana*, Vol. 34, No. 20. Nov. 1-15, 1990, pp. 4-5.

Mishra, S.K. and Puri, V.K., *Development and Planning: Theory and Practice*, (Bombay, Himalaya, 1986).

Moddie, A.D. *Explorations in Management Development* (New Delhi, AIMA, 1976).

Myrdal, G., *Asian Drama* (Penguin, 1963).

Nadler, L., *Developing Human Resources* (Texas, Concepts, 1979).

Nadler, L., *The Handbook of Human Resources Development* (John Willey, 1984).

Nallagounden, A.M. 'Investment in Education in India' *Journal of Human Resource,* Vol. 2, No. 3, Summer- 1967, pp. 347-58.

Nandedkar, V.G., 'Human Resource: Both an End and Means', *Yojana,* Vol. 34, Nos. 1 and 2, Jan. 26, 1990, pp. 50-53.

National Council of Educational Research and Training. *The Fourth All India Education Survey* (New Delhi, NCERT, 1982).

Niland, John R., *The Production of Manpower Specialists: A Volume of Selected Papers* (New York, Cornell University, 1971).

Nurkse, R., *Problems of Capital Formation in Underdeveloped Countries,* (New Delhi, OUP, 1973).

OECD, *Education in OECD Developing Countries: Trends and Perspectives,* (France, OECD, 1974).

Ota, Masao. 'Quantitative Method For the Planning of Human Resource Development', *Research Bulletin of the National Institute for Educational Research,* No. 11, 1972, pp. 25-41.

Panchamukhi, V.R. Leading Issues in Human Resource Development in India' in P.R. Brahmananda, and V.R. Panchamukhi, (Ed), *Development Process of the Indian Economy,* (Bombay, Himalaya, 1987), pp. 1060-1108.

Pandit, H.N., *Measurement of Cost Productivity and Efficiency of Education* (Delhi, NCERT, 1969).

Pandit, H.N., 'A Study in Unit Costs at School Stage in India: A Design of the Research Project (Pandit, H.N. (Ed), *1969, op. cit.,* pp. 3-13.

Panigrahi, D., 'Human Resource Development in Business Administration', B.L. Mathur, (Ed), *op. cit.*

Parkash, Shri., *Educational System of India: An Econometric Study* (Delhi, Concept, 1978).

Parminder Kaur, and Singh, Bhawdeep, 'Human Resource Development in Rural Punjab' in *U.G.C. National Seminar* held at G.K.I.A.S. in Rural Development (Punjabi University Campus), Damdama Sahib, 22-23, Feb., 1991.

Patel, S.J., 'Educational Miracle in The Third World', *Economic and Political Weekly*, Vol. XX, No. 31, August 3, 1985, pp. 1312-17.

Patil, V.T. and Patil, B.C., *Problems in Indian Education* (New Delhi, Oxford and IBH, 1982).

Perlman, R., *The Economics of Education: Conceptual Problems and Policy Issues* (McGraw Hill, 1973).

Paillai, S.S., 'Educational System and Social Structure', *Educational India*, Vol. 9, March, 1973.

Planning Commission., *The Sixth Five Year Plan: 1980-85* (New Delhi, Government of India).

Planning Commission., *The First Year Plan: 1951-56* (Delhi, Government of India).

Psachorapoulos, G., *Earnings and Education in OECD Countries* (Paris, OECD, 1973).

Psachorapoulos, G., 'Education and Development—A Review', *Pigmy Economic Review*, Monthly Economic Journal of the Syndicate Bank, Oct. 88, Vol. 34, No. 3.

Punit, A.E., *Social System in Rural India* (New Delhi, Sterling, 1978).

Radhakrishnan, S., *The Creative Life.*

Index